ALASTAIR SAWDAY'S
SPECIAL PLACES TO STAY

£14.99/$23.95

£11.99/$21.95

£11.99/$21.95

Credit card orders (free p&p for UK orders) 01275 395431
www.specialplacestostay.com

In US: credit card orders (800) 243-0495, 9am-5pm EST,
24-hour fax (800) 820-2329 www.globepequot.com

Fourth edition
Copyright © 2007
Alastair Sawday Publishing Co. Ltd

Published in 2007
Alastair Sawday Publishing,
The Old Farmyard,
Yanley Lane, Long Ashton
Bristol BS41 9LR
Tel: +44 (0)1275 395430
Fax: +44 (0)1275 393388
Email: info@specialplacestostay.com
Web: www.specialplacestostay.com

A catalogue record for this book is
available from the British Library.

Paper and Printing: We have sought the lowest
possible ecological 'footprint' from the production
of this book, using super-efficient machinery,
vegetable inks and high environmental standards.
Our printer is ISO 14001-registered.

Design:
Caroline King

Maps & Mapping:
Maidenhead Cartographic Services Ltd

Printing:
Butler & Tanner, Frome, UK

UK Distribution:
Penguin UK, 80 Strand, London

ISBN-13: 978-1-901970-83-8

ALASTAIR SAWDAY'S
SPECIAL PLACES TO STAY

PORTUGAL

Contents

Back Page

Photo istock.com

Alastair Sawday Publishing

Our main aim is to publish beautiful guidebooks but, for us, the question of who we are is also important. For who we are shapes the books, the books shape your holidays, and thus are shaped the lives of people who own these 'special places'. So we are trying to be a little more than 'just a publishing company'.

New eco offices

In January 2006 we moved into our new eco offices. With super-insulation, underfloor heating, a wood-pellet boiler, solar panels and a rainwater tank, we have a working environment benign to ourselves and to the environment. Lighting is low-energy, dark corners are lit by sun-pipes and one building is of green oak. Carpet tiles are from Herdwick sheep in the Lake District.

Environmental & ethical policies

We make many other gestures: company cars run on gas or recycled cooking oil; kitchen waste is composted and other waste recycled; cycling and car-sharing are encouraged; the company only buys organic or local food; we don't accept web links with companies we consider unethical; we bank with the ethical Triodos Bank.

We have used recycled paper for some books but have settled on selecting paper and printing for their low energy use. Our printer is British and ISO14001-certified and together we will work to reduce our environmental impact.

In 2005 we won a Business Commitment to the Environment Award and in April 2006 we won a Queen's Award for Enterprise in the Sustainable Development category. All this has boosted our resolve to promote our green policies. Our flagship gesture, however, is carbon offsetting; we calculate our carbon emissions and plant trees to compensate and support projects overseas that plant trees or reduce carbon use.

Carbon offset

SCAD in South India, supports the poorest of the poor. The money we send to offset our carbon emissions will be used to encourage village tree planting and, eventurally, low-carbon technologies. Why India? Because the money goes a long way and admin costs are very low. www.salt-of-the-earth.org.uk

Ethics

But why, you may ask, take these things so seriously? You are just a little publishing company, for heaven's sake! Well, is there any good argument for not taking them seriously? The world, by the admission of the vast majority of scientists, is in trouble. If we do not change our ways urgently we will

Who are we?

doom the planet and all its creatures – whether innocent or not – to a variety of possible catastrophes. To maintain the status quo is unacceptable. Business does much of the damage and should undo it, and provide new models.

Pressure on companies to produce Corporate Social Responsibility policies is mounting. We are trying to keep ahead of it all, yet still to be as informal and human as possible – the antithesis of 'corporate'.

The books – and a dilemma
So, we have created fine books that do good work. They promote authenticity, individuality and good local and organic food – a far cry from corporate culture. Rural economies, pubs, small farms, villages and hamlets all benefit. However, people use fossil fuel to get there. Should we aim to get our readers to offset their own carbon emissions, and the B&B and hotel owners too?

We are gradually introducing green ideas into the books: the Fine Breakfast scheme that highlights British and Irish B&B owners who use local and organic food; celebrating those who make an extra environmental effort; gently encouraging the use of public transport, cycling and walking. Last year we published Green Places to Stay focusing on responsible travel and eco-properties around the globe.

Our Fragile Earth series
The 'hard' side of our environmental publishing is the Fragile Earth series: The Little Earth Book, The Little Food Book and The Little Money Book. They consist of bite-sized essays, polemical, hard-hitting and well researched. They are a 'must have' for anyone who seeks clarity about some of the key issues of our time. Last year we have also published One Planet Living.

Lastly – what is special?
The notion of 'special' is at the heart of what we do, and highly subjective. We discuss this in the introduction. We take huge pleasure from finding people and places that do their own thing – brilliantly; places that are unusual and follow no trends; places of peace and beauty; people who are kind and interesting – and genuine.

We seem to have touched a nerve with thousands of readers; they obviously want to stay in special places rather than the dull corporate monstrosities that have disfigured so many of our cities and towns. Life is too short to be wasted in the wrong places. A night in a special place can be a transforming experience.

Alastair Sawday

Acknowledgements

The last edition of this book was put together by the redoubtable Laura Kinch, with powerful support from others. Laura got off to another determined and inspired start on this edition but was laid low by such a grim bout of illness that her place had to be taken by colleagues. Jackie King came to the rescue and skilfully managed the final months, ably abetted by Florence Oldfield. Carol Dymond has again given solid support to the project as have all our office staff, writers and inspectors listed, but particular thanks are due to Elise Parsons for so calmly stepping in to take over an inspection trip at the very last minute.

Alastair Sawday

Series Editor Alastair Sawday

Editor Laura Kinch

Editorial Director Annie Shillito

Writing Jo Boissevain, Viv Cripps, Abigail Hole, Matthew Hilton-Dennis, Laura Kinch, Helen Pickles

Inspections Carol Dymond, Marie Golding, Eva Graburn, Carlos Jardim, Laura Kinch, Elise Parsons, Alethea Tonner

Accounts **Bridget Bishop,** Jessica Britton, Christine Buxton, Sandra Hasell, Sally Ranahan

Editorial **Jackie King,** Jo Boissevain, Florence Oldfield, Maria Serrano, Rebecca Stevens, Danielle Williams

Production **Julia Richardson,** Rachel Coe, Tom Germain, Rebecca Thomas

Sales & Marketing & PR Andreea Petre Goncalves, Sarah Bolton

Web & IT **Russell Wilkinson,** Chris Banks, Isabelle Deakin, Joe Green, Brian Kimberling

Previous Editors John Dalton, Guy Hunter-Watts

A word from Alastair Sawday

For a country so long at the centre of world events, Portugal can seem strangely removed from them. She is, of course, on the physical edge of the continent, hemmed in by a vast and re-energised Spain. But, she is beginning to find her new voice.

Portugal is also a richly rewarding country for visitors, especially those with a little curiosity. It is barely possible to be in Lisbon without being aware of its glorious (and inglorious) past, its place once at the centre of a vast empire. It was, some thought, the loveliest of all Europe's capitals, before the disastrous fire that reduced so much of it to ruins; but the re-building has produced wonderful results. It is now a curious mix of styles and moods, endearingly human in scale but with buildings as mighty as any in Europe.

Wherever you go in the land you will be struck by the quiet dignity of the Portuguese. They have often shown me grace and manners out of favour in our times, and always kindness. They are, perhaps, less hectic than the rest of us, less caught up in the frenzy that is modern consumerism.

Go and judge for yourselves; there is no better way of getting to know the Portuguese than by brandishing this remarkable book as your entry to her fascinating and varied houses and hotels. You will also be introduced to friendships with her people. For we have within these pages a delightful crowd; you could not possibly gather them all under your wing in a lifetime of conviviality.

Alastair Sawday

Photo Tom Germain

Introduction

AN INSPIRING MIX OF OLD AND NEW, OF DEEPLY TRADITIONAL HOMES AND FUNKY BOUTIQUE HOTELS...

The winds of change are rolling in off the sea in Portugal, rustling through the forests, racing over the plains and sweeping across the mountains.

Prime Minister José Socrates is on a mission to raise the country's profile – to elevate 'poor old Portugal' to a nation that is as prosperous as the Portugal of old. His aim? To stem unemployment and turn Portugal into a nation that attracts more foreign investment and tourism. Portugal's economy has been in the doldrums in recent years and, despite a necessary tightening of the country's collective belt, there is now a groundswell of support for what Senhor Socrates is trying to achieve. Many Portuguese are anticipating a revival of their nation's fortunes.

Two of the country's new initiatives are set to have a major environmental impact. Firstly, the building of a vast wind farm in the Minho valley into which €340 million are being poured. Secondly, investment of cash into tourist areas other than the Algarve – which attracts an incredible, and increasingly unsustainable number of visitors a year. Other recognised jewels in Portugal's crown are: the northern coastal areas of Minho, the Alqueva lake and dam in Alentejo, the Serra da Estrela mountains, the Douro wine valley, and the historic town of Porto. All will receive injections of cash to lure more of the 24 million foreign spenders each year. As for natural wealth, Portugal has stacks of it: sun, wind, water and biomass sufficient to enable the country to meet its own energy needs – and 800 kilometres of coastline, 220 days of sun a year and a culture that looks to the past with respect and to the future with vigour.

This book is filled with an inspiring mix of old and new, of deeply traditional homes and funky boutique hotels, of noble families with centuries of tradition running through their veins, and of young hosts blazing trails, spotting niche markets and offering an easy-going flexibility.

Photo left Quintassential Holiday Cottages, entry 172
Photo right Quinta da Bouça d'Arques, entry 5

Introduction

For a relatively small country, the range of properties is huge: cottages and castles, palaces and pousadas, even the odd windmill or coach house. And there's a pleasingly wide range of prices, too. With this guide you can orchestrate your way through Portugal, perhaps choosing 'cheap and cheerful' one day, pampering indulgence the next: staying in a regal bed in an imposing pousada, or in a beach cabana within sound of crashing waves.

Shun those foreign-owned golf complexes, pass those ubiquitous travel lodges by, and meet the real Portugal! We are proud to promote places to stay that actively benefit the country's economy. We have non-Portuguese owners within these pages too, but we can vouch for their passion for their adopted country; they employ local staff, immerse themselves in the local economy and are ever-keen to promote the best of Portugal.

How we choose our places
We are fortunate that you often share your discoveries with us, that you write with enthusiasm and that you inspire us to inspect the places you have discovered. We are hugely grateful for your tips, so please keep them coming.

Our inspectors, too, know their patch – most live in Portugal and are integrated into Portuguese life, unearthing little gems to add to our stable and alerting us to those against whom we should bolt the door.

What to expect
This guide to mainland Portugal and Madeira contains B&Bs, self-catering houses, small properties and pousadas. Many B&Bs and hotels also have self-catering options – we've mentioned this on their entries and flagged them accordingly on the map pages.

Types of property
There are many clues as to what to expect in the property name alone so we thought it worth explaining them all, the obvious and the not-so-obvious.

Albergaria an upmarket inn
Cabana a hut
Casa a house, old or new
Castelo a castle
Estalagem an inn, more expensive than an albergaria
Herdade a large farm or estate
Monte a long, low Alentejo farmhouse, usually on top of a hill
Paço a palace or country house
Palacio a palace or country house that is grander than a paço
Pensão a guest house, the Portuguese equivalent of a bed and breakfast, although breakfast is not always included in the price
Quinta a country estate or villa; in the Douro wine-growing area it

often refers to a vineyard
Fortaleza a fort
Residencial a town guest house, slightly more expensive than a pensão, usually serving breakfast
Solar a manor house

Tourist definitions are listed below; you'll often see these marked on blue road signs.

Turismo de habitacão B&B in a stately home
Turismo rural a rustic house
Agroturismo B&B on a farm
Casa de campo simple rural private house
Hotel rural a country hotel

B&Bs

You'll find a huge variety of houses calling themselves B&Bs; the common factor is that in all of them you stay as a guest in a private home. You eat either at the dining table, perhaps with your hosts, or with the other guests. And even if your bedroom is grand with antique furniture and parquet floor, the overall feel and welcome will be personal. The Portuguese tourist board often describes this type of house as a 'turismo de habitacão'; it may well be the largest house in the village and may even have its own chapel. A 'turismo rural' is also a B&B but is usually more rustic. You will often find self-catering apartments on the same plot of land, too.

Photo Quinta do Barriero, entry 114

An 'agroturismo' is a B&B on a working farm, and the outbuildings are often converted to take self-catering guests too. Farmer-owners often offer good value short breaks so do check when booking. We give as many details as possible in this guide but each property's web site will be more illuminating – although obviously not all of them appear in English.

A 'residencial' is an urban B&B, usually set right in the heart of a town and with hotel-like facilities.

Hotels

Those we choose normally have fewer than 50 rooms; many are family-run with friendly staff and in old buildings, others have a 'chic boutique' feel. An 'albergaria' is a small, upmarket inn which is usually excellent value for money but not generally as smart as a hotel.

Introduction

Pousadas

This is the name given to a collection of Living History Hotels in restored historic buildings such as monasteries, convents and castles. Often grand and imposing, pousadas can give a real flavour of old Portugal and the best will have good restaurants serving traditional dishes using local produce. An added bonus is that many stand in the most beautiful spots in the country, and have spectacular views. The feel is definitely more hotel than B&B. As with all our places, we have visited and found special all those pousadas that appear in this guide.

Depending on the season, current room prices in pousadas range from €90-€380: pricey at the top end, but the profit goes towards an ongoing programme of renovation and regeneration of some of the most significant buildings in the country. The web site www.pousadas.pt regularly features special deals and discounts. A couple of examples (subject to change) are: a 40% discount for the over 55s at some pousadas, discounts for those under 30 and three nights for the price of two in participating pousadas. There is also a 'passport' which entitles you to four nights at any pousada for a set rate.

The pousadas in this guide belong to a group of just over 40 hotels set up by the government in the 1940s. The Pestana Group deals with marketing and promotions. For further information contact:
Pousadas de Portugal ,
Avenida Santa Joana Princesa n° 10,
1749-090 Lisboa
Tel: +351 218 442001
Fax: +351 218 442085
email: guest@pousadas.pt
www.pousadas.pt

The official UK representative for Portuguese pousadas is Keytel International. For enquiries and bookings contact:
Keytel International,
402 Edgware Road, London W2 1ED
Tel: 0207 616 0300
Fax: 0207 616 0317
email: keytel@keytel.co.uk
www.keytel.co.uk

Photo above Quinta de Alcaídaria – Mórentry, entry 103
Photo right Casa de Terena entry 131

Introduction

Green entries

Many of our owners are making monumental efforts to run their homes and hotels in an environmentally-friendly way – going beyond merely recycling the recyclable. In this guide we've highlighted six owners who have high regard for the environment, wildlife and sustainability. Their entry numbers are 14, 17, 78, 145, 148, 167.

How to use this book
Map

If you know in which region you want to stay, our maps are your best guide; if you only consult the regional headings in the book you may miss a gem just over the border in a neighbouring region.

Numbered properties are flagged on the map and coloured to show whether they are B&Bs/hotels (red) or self-catering properties (blue). Dual-coloured flags show that they do both. We have also included one place just across the Spanish border.

Rooms

We try to give an accurate breakdown of the type of bedrooms available stating whether they are single, double, twin, triple, family rooms or suites and whether they are in the main building or in apartments or cottages. Extra beds can often be added for children and many twin beds can be zipped together to make doubles. Ask your host for more details and you'll find they often have a flexible approach, particularly to families and their needs.

Bathrooms

The vast majority of bedrooms in this book are en suite. Only if a bedroom has a shared or private bathroom do we list bathroom details. Each entry should give you all the info you need but there are subtleties of punctuation so read carefully!

Prices

Prices for B&Bs and hotels are per night for two people and give a range from low season to high season. Self-catering prices are given per night and per week. But prices may shift – usually upwards – so do check when booking. Many owners offer special deals for off-season or longer stays. The 'singles' price given is the price for a single room or for the single occupancy of a double room.

Weddings, conferences and courses

We try to say when a hotel or B&B is a popular wedding or conference place; in any event, it is best to ask if a large party is likely to be present when you book. The same goes for courses. More places are encouraging relaxation, cookery or painting breaks and you may well find your peaceful haven does not turn out to be quite as peaceful as you'd expected. Pick up the phone and check.

Symbols

There is an explanation of these on the inside back cover of the book. Use them as a guide, not as a statement of fact. If an owner does not have the symbol that you're looking for, it's worth discussing your needs; the Portuguese generally love to please. Most owners speak some English – and there is an 'English spoken' symbol (Hello).

Quick reference indices

At the back of the book is a quick reference section to direct you to places that meet particular requirements.

Practical Matters

Bookings

It is best to confirm your booking in writing. Often you will need to pay a deposit, the equivalent of one night's stay or 30% of a week's holiday. You can do this by credit card (if the owner has the ⊟ symbol), personal cheque or bank transfer. If you make your booking by telephone, many hotels will ask you for a credit card number as an insurance against cancellation. Do make sure that you have written confirmation of all you have discussed, ask for detailed directions and be clear about your dining arrangements/requirements in

Photo Casa do Paço de Ilhas, entry 71

smaller places. Book well ahead if you plan to be in Portugal during school holidays. August is a good month to avoid the busy beaches and to head for the remoter places in this book.

Portugal is in the same time zone as the UK but remember if you pop across the border to Spain, it is one hour ahead.

Arrivals

Many city hotels will only hold a reservation until the early evening, even if you booked months in advance. So warn them if you are planning to arrive late. It remains law that you should register on arrival but hotels have no right to keep your passport.

Tipping

Tipping is not as widespread in Portugal as in the UK and US. However, the more expensive restaurants do expect a 10% service charge, if it is not already included.

Introduction

Public holidays & festivals

In Portugal many shops, businesses and restaurants in all but the busiest areas are closed at Easter, Christmas and New Year, and on the following public holidays:

Feb/March: Carnival Tuesday (day before Ash Wednesday)
March/April: Good Friday
25 April: Liberty Day, commemorating the 1974 Revolution
1 May: Labour Day
May/June: Corpus Christi (ninth Tuesday after Easter)
10 June: Portugal Day; Camões & the Communities Day
15 August: The Feast of the Assumption
5 October: Republic Day, commemorating the 1910 declaration of the Portuguese Republic
1 November: All Saints Day
1 December: Independence Day, commemorating the 1640 restoration of independence from Spain
8 December: Feast of the Immaculate Conception

Telephones

Calling Portugal from another country:

From UK: 00 351 then the number.
From USA: 011 351 then the number.

Landline numbers begin with 2, mobile phone numbers with 9.

Photo Monte dos Pensamentos, entry 123

As well as public phone boxes (for which you can buy phone cards in most newsagents) and phone boxes inside post offices (look for Correios), virtually every café has a phone for which customers pay the impulsos used, counted on a meter. Many owners answer the phone with "estou" (which, literally translated, means "I'm ready").

Electricity

Virtually all sockets have 220/240 AC voltage (usually 2-pin). Pack an adaptor if you are travelling with a laptop, mobile or – a boon in summer – a bedside fan.

Driving

The maps in this guide give an approximate idea of where places are; use them with an up-to-date detailed road map for navigation. Obviously it's best to avoid driving around cities and towns at rush hours on and around public holidays; and in August when there is a mass exodus to the countryside and the coast. It is compulsory to have a spare set of bulbs, a warning triangle, a fire extinguisher and a basic first aid kit in the car.

It is an offence to drive without having your driving licence on you. Remember that foreign number plates attract attention in the big cities so never leave your car with valuables inside.

Introduction

The following are general guidelines: Auto-estradas – toll motorways (portagems), usually with two to three lanes – are indicated by blue signs and road numbers preceded by 'A' and are generally shown on maps with a bold double red line. Make sure you take the toll ticket.

Itinário-principal (IP) & Itiniário complementar (IC) are the main non-toll roads; sometimes the road names change mid-route. Estradas Nacionais (national two-lane roads) are usually prefixed by an N.

Petrol is more expensive in Portugal than in the UK (and much more expensive than in the USA). Don't wait until you hit red on the gauge before filling up as you can often go for many miles (even on the biggest roads) without coming across a station.

Public transport

You can get almost everywhere by train or bus. Trains are inexpensive and some lines very scenic, but it's usually quicker to go by bus, especially for shorter journeys. Buses marked 'carreiras' (or CR) are the slow local buses. 'Expressos' are direct buses between large towns and 'rápidas' are fast regional buses. One of the quick reference indices at the back of the book tells you the entry numbers for those properties you can easily reach by public transport. Make sure you discuss finer details with your host.

Food

It can be inexpensive to eat out in Portugal. The set meal, 'ementa turistica', may offer a small choice, while à la carte, 'á lista', is a full choice. The dish of the day, 'prato do dia', is usually a local speciality and helpings can be enormous. It is perfectly fine to ask for a 'meia dose', half portion, or for two adults to ask for 'uma dose', a single portion to share.

At virtually any restaurant in Portugal you will be given bits to nibble before your meal arrives – most often olives, chouriço, sardine spread and bread – but you will be charged for whatever you eat. If you don't want it, just say so.

Bacalhão, salted cod, is the national dish: there are said to be 365 different ways of preparing it! Pork, as in Spain, is also popular; the homemade vegetable soups are often good and so is fresh fish near the coast.

Many Special Places have restaurants or make authentic local dishes. The 🍎 symbol shows those places that can provide vegetarian dinners – a welcome plus in a mainly carnivorous country.

Environment

Portugal is becoming more 'green' and most places have a recycling centre you can use.
For information about the environment in Portugal check out www.naturlink.pt

Portuguese Tourist Offices

UK: 11 Belgrave Square, London SW1X 8PP
Tel: 0845 3551212
tourism@portugaloffice.org.uk
www.visitportugal.com

USA: 4th Floor, 590 Fifth Avenue, New York, NY 10036-4785
Tel: 212 354 4403
tourism@portugal.org
www.portugalinsite.com

Subscriptions

Owners pay to appear in this guide. Their fee goes towards the high costs of inspecting and producing an all-colour book and maintaining a sophisticated web site. We only include places that we like and find special for one reason or another. It is not possible for anyone to buy their way onto these pages.

Internet

www.specialplacestostay.com has online pages for all the special places featured here and from all our other books — around 5,000 in total. There's a searchable database, a taster of the write-ups and colour photos. And look out for our dedicated web site on self-catering in England, Scotland and Wales, www.special-escapes.co.uk.
For more details, see the back of the book.

Disclaimer

We make no claims to pure objectivity in choosing our Special Places. They are here because we like them. Our opinions and tastes are ours alone and this book is a statement of them; we hope that you will share them. We have done our utmost to get our facts right and we apologise unreservedly for any errors that may have crept in.

We do not check such things as fire alarms, swimming pool security or any other regulation with which owners of properties receiving paying guests should comply. This is the responsibility of the owners.

Feedback

Feedback from you is invaluable and we always act upon comments, which may be sent by letter or email to info@sawdays.co.uk.
Or you can visit our web site and write to us from there. With your help and our own inspections we can maintain our reputation for dependability. Please be patient with us at busy times; it can be difficult to respond immediately.

Introduction

Poor reports are followed up with owners: we need to hear both sides of the story. Really worrying reports lead to incognito visits, after which we may exclude a place. As a general rule, try to deal with issues on the spot – most owners will appreciate your honesty and the chance to fix things.

Owners are also informed when we receive positive reports about them. If you recommend a new place and it goes in the guide because of your recommendation you receive a free copy of the edition in which it first appears.

So tell us if your stay has been a joy or not, if the atmosphere was great or stuffy, whether the owners or staff were cheery or bored. We aim to celebrate human kindness, fine architecture, real food, history and landscape, and hope that these books may be your passport to memorable experiences.

Photo Monte Saraz, entry 132

SPAIN

Viana do Castelo

MINHO

Braga

Chaves

Bragança

TRÁS-OS-MONTES E ALTO DOURO

Vila Real

Oporto (Porto)

DOURO LITORAL

BEIRA ALTA

ATLANTIC OCEAN

Aveiro

Viseu

Guarda

Coimbra

Covilhã

BEIRA LITORAL

BEIRA BAIXA

Marinha Grande

Castelo Branco

Caldas da Rainha

Santarém

Portalegre

ESTREMADURA

RIBATEJO

ALTO ALENTEJO

LISBON

Setúbal

Évora

SPAIN

Beja

BAIXO ALENTEJO

ALGARVE

Faro

MADEIRA

Funchal

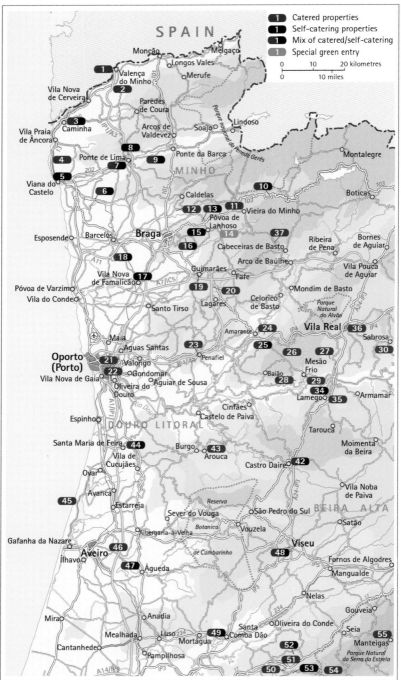

SPAIN

1 Catered properties
1 Self-catering properties
1 Mix of catered/self-catering
1 Special green entry

0   10   20 kilometres
0   10 miles

Monção
Melgaço
Longos Vales
Valença
do Minho
Merufe
1
Vila Nova
de Cerveira
2
Paredes
de Coura
Arcos de
Valdevez
Soajo
Lindoso
3
Caminha
Parque nacional da Peneda Gerês
Vila Praia
de Âncora
8
Ponte da Barca
Montalegre
4
Ponte de Lima
9
5
7
MINHO
Viana do
Castelo
6
Caldelas
10
Boticas
12 13 11 Vieira do Minho
Póvoa de
Lanhoso
Esposende
Barcelos
Braga
15
14
37
Ribeira
de Pena
Bornes
de Aguiar
16
Cabeceiras de Basto
18
Arco de Baúlhe
Vila Nova
de Famalicão
17
Guimarães
Fafe
Vila Pouca
de Aguiar
Póvoa de Varzim
19
20
Mondim de Basto
Vila do Conde
Lagares
Celorico
de Basto
Parque
Natural
do Alvão
Santo Tirso
Maia
Águas Santas
23
Amarante
24
Vila Real
36
Sabrosa
Oporto
(Porto)
21
Valongo
Penafiel
25
26
27
30
22
Gondomar
Aguiar de Sousa
Baião
Mesão
Frio
Vila Nova de Gaia
Oliveira do
Douro
28
29
Espinho
DOURO LITORAL
Cinfães
Castelo de Paiva
34
Lamego
35
Armamar
Tarouca
Santa Maria de Feira
44
Burgo
43
Arouca
Moimenta
da Beira
Vila de
Cucujães
Castro Daire
42
Ovar
Avanca
Vila Noba
de Paiva
45
Estarreja
Reserva
BEIRA ALTA
Sever do Vouga
São Pedro do Sul
Gafanha da Nazare
Botanica
Vouzela
Satão
Albergaria-a-Velha
Ilhavo
Aveiro
46
de Cambarinho
Viseu
Fornos de Algodres
47
Águeda
48
Mangualde
Nelas
Gouveia
Mira
Anadia
Oliveira do Conde
Seia
55
Mealhada
Luso
49
Santa
Comba Dão
Manteigas
Cantanhede
Mortágua
52
Parque Natural
da Serra da Estrela
Pampilhosa
51
50
53
54

Map 2

25

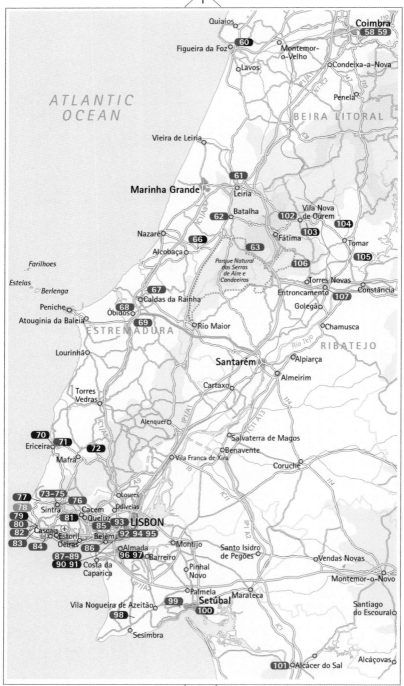

Map 4

Coja
Arganil
Covilhã
Penamacor
Fundão 57
Castanheira de Pera
BEIRA BAIXA
Oleiros
Idanha-a-Nova
64 Serta
Castelo Branco
Vila Velha de Rodão
65
Abrantes
Gavião
108
Alpalhão
Castelo de Vide 111
Marvão 112
110 114 113
SPAIN
109
Crato
Portalegre 115
Parque Natural da Serra de São Mamede
Ponte de Sor
116
117
Arronches
Avis
Fronteira
Monforte
Santa Eulália
Mora
Campo Major
Pavia
ALTO ALENTEJO
118
Sousel
124 Estremoz
Elvas
Vimiero
129
123 Borba
126 127
119
125
Vila Viçosa
Arraiolos
128
122
Redondo
120 121
130 131 Terena
Évora
Montoito
132
133
Reguengos de Monsaraz
Aguiar
Mourão

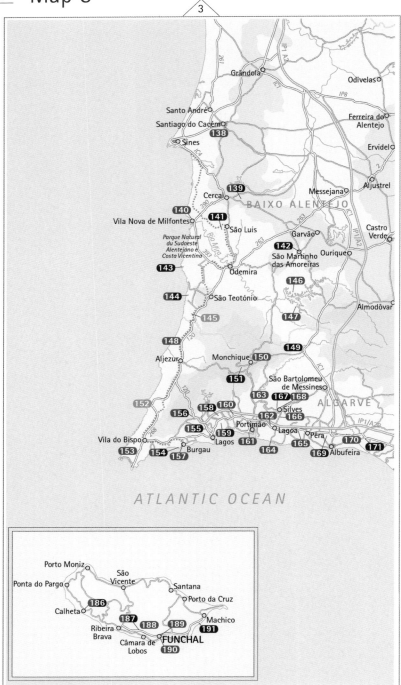

3

Grândola
Odivelas
IP1 A2
IP8
Santo André
Santiago do Cacém
138
Ferreira do Alentejo
Sines
Ervidel
Aljustrel
139
Cercal
Messejana
BAIXO ALENTEJO
140
141
Vila Nova de Milfontes
São Luis
Garvão
Castro Verde
Parque Natural
du Sudoeste
Alentejano e
Costa Vicentina
142
São Martinho
das Amoreiras
Ourique
IP1/A2
143
Odemira
146
144
São Teotónio
147
145
Almodôvar
148
Aljezur
Monchique
150
149
151
152
São Bartolomeu
de Messines
163
167 168
ALGARVÉ
156
158 160
Silves
162
166
IP1/A2
155
Portimão
Lagoa
Pêra
170
171
Vila do Bispo
159
Lagos
161
164
165
169 Albufeira
153
154 157
Burgau

ATLANTIC OCEAN

Porto Moniz
São Vicente
Ponta do Pargo
Santana
Porto da Cruz
186
Calheta
187
188
189
Machico
Ribeira Brava
191
Câmara de Lobos
FUNCHAL
190

Map 6

4

Viana do Alentejo
136
135 Alvito
134 Portel
IP2

Cuba

Moura
Safara
Barrancos

Beringel
Beja
137
Santo Aleixo da Restauração

Rio Guadiana

Santa Clara de Louredo
Serpa
Vila Verde de Ficalho
IP8

IP2
Trindade
Aldeia Nova de São Bento

BAIXO ALENTEJO

122

São Marcos da Ataboeira

Mina de São Domingos

SPAIN

Mértola
Parque Natural do Vale Guadiana

Alcoutim
122

Castro Marim
IP1/A22

São Brás de Alportel **181**
173
Loulé
174 **175**
182

172
176 Estôl
180
Tavira
183–185

178
177
179

Faro Olhão
Parque Natural da Ria Formosa

ATLANTIC OCEAN

Minho

Photo Laura Kinch

Pousada de Valença do Minho

São Teotónio, Baluarte Socorro, 4930-619 Valença do Minho, Minho

The hillfort of Valença do Minho boldly stands on the north-western frontier with Spain, staring out at the fortress in Tui just metres from the river border. Enter crenellated gates clearly designed for horses and carts. Today the cobbled streets are wide enough for a car — just — and are merry with streetsellers, tourists and banter. Push through the throng to the far end of the fortress and you enter the peaceful haven of the pousada. The building is modern and not overly inspirational but we include it because of its position within this fabulous fortress — and its views. Bedroom furnishings are on the conservative side but no matter — they are very comfortable and have sparkling white bathrooms. Ask for a room with a view towards the south. The restaurant probably has the best choice of regional food within the city walls and the terrace and lounge buzzes around teatime. After dinner, retire to one of the lounges with sofas to sink into, modern art on the walls and gentle music. A great stop-off point if driving to or from the ferry in Santander.

rooms	18: 7 doubles, 11 twins.
price	€120–€180. Special offers available – see web site.
meals	Dinner, 3 courses, €30.
closed	Rarely.
directions	In Valença, follow signs for Fortaleza. Go into fortress walls & follow signs for Pousada São Teorónio.

Senhor António Neiva

tel	+351 251 800260
fax	+351 251 824397
email	recepcao.steotonio@pousadas.pt
web	www.pousadas.pt

Hotel

Map 1 Entry 1

Pousada de Vila Nova de Cerveira

Dom Diniz, Largo do Terreiro, 4920-296 V. Nova de Cerveira, Minho

Come in September and join in the harvest. Eveyone carries their crop to the main square where villagers help to separate the corn heads; then the party starts, and lasts all weekend. Within the old town walls is a castle – whence great river views – then, up tiny cobbled streets, this 13th-century manor house, the pousada. It's made up not of one grand building, but, charmingly, of several little converted houses, some with terraces, some with views. The young staff are friendly and helpful, happy to park your car and organise your baggage. Bedrooms have toile de Jouy fabrics with Portuguese scenes for bedcovers and curtains, and there are dried corn sheaves, still-life prints and blue and cream rugs for decoration. Sparkling bathrooms have deep tubs and thick robes. After dinner, settle down in the cosy bar with a drink and a game or two. The sea is ten kilometres away but you can feel it, and there's a boat that will take you down the wide Minho river to the coast. A dizzy array of good things at breakfast – including champagne, should you be feeling celebratory.

rooms	29: 6 doubles, 18 twins, 2 triples, 3 suites.
price	€150-€230. Special offers available - see web site.
meals	Dinner, 3 courses, from €30.
closed	Rarely.
directions	In Vila Nova de Cerveira, follow signs for pousada. Unload in front of hotel.

Senhor Marco Santos

tel	+351 251 708120
fax	+351 251 708129
email	recepcao.ddinis@pousadas.pt
web	www.pousadas.pt

Hotel

Map 1 Entry 2

Casa de Esteiró

Vilarelho, 4910-605 Caminha, Minho

A magical old house that reflects the warm, outgoing personalities of owners José and Maria, and a rich experience from the moment you arrive. This late 18th-century house is extremely handsome and decorated with antiques and fine furniture – traditional Portuguese as well as finds from the owners' years abroad in the diplomatic service. The gallery is long, with masses of comfortable seating, beautiful cushions, porcelain and paintings, plus a lovely granite fireplace. The library is exquisite, and there is a small chapel off it (ask about the altar carried by Great Grandfather during the Peninsular War). Bedrooms too have Portuguese and foreign furnishings, the suite is particularly special; all are fresh with garden flowers. Breakfast can be served either in your room or in the formal dining room, lined with beautiful ceramic dishes. Outside: a good pool and a garden with many specimen trees (planted by an earlier owner, Viscount Negrelos), which thrive in this Minho climate... and some delightful quiet areas for sitting and listening to the running water and birds. *Minimum stay two nights.*

rooms	2 + 3: 1 suite, 1 studio for 2. 3 apartments for 2-4.
price	€90-€100. Singles €65-€80. Apartments €130.
meals	Restaurant 200m.
closed	Rarely.
directions	From Viana do Castelo to Valença on N13. In Caminha, right at 1st sign for the Centre & Turismo de Habitaçâo. At T-junc. right at sign Casa de Esteiró. On right; ring bell.

José Manuel & Maria Villas-Boas

tel	+351 258 721333
fax	+351 258 921356
email	casaesteiro@iol.pt
web	www.ciberguia.pt/casa-esteiro

B&B & Self-catering

Map 1 Entry 3

Casa Santa Filomena

Estrada de Cabanas, Afife, 4900-012 Viana do Castelo, Minho

A grand entrance gate beckons you in to the Casa Santa Filomena, a solid, stonewalled building that was built in the 1920s. It is tucked into a quiet corner of an already quiet village; peace is assured. When we visited in early spring the old wisteria was a riot of tumbling lilac and mauve, as pretty a welcome as you could wish for. A high wall runs around the property; it girdles a small vineyard where vinho verde grapes are grown. Elsewhere the profusion of flowers is heady proof of the microclimate that this part of the Minho enjoys. It seems as if anything will grow here, and your breakfast juice will be from the oranges in the garden. Bedrooms are rather functional but perfectly clean and comfortable. Your hosts and their staff are extremely helpful; José himself has a passion for collecting and restoring carriages. When he's around, ask to see them: they are a delight. This is a charming and secluded spot, and good value. Among other diversions, a swimming pool and tennis courts are a kilometre away, and wonderful beaches not much further. *Minimum stay three nights.*

rooms	5: 4 twins/doubles, 1 suite.
price	€50–€55. Suite €60.
meals	Restaurants nearby. B&B accepts BYO wine.
closed	Rarely.
directions	From Valença to Viana, 1st left to Afife. From Viana 1st right. At square in centre of Afife turn inland/right (Estrada de Cabanas). House up hill on left at 1st fork.

José & Mary Street Kendall

tel	+351 258 981619
fax	+351 226 175936
email	soc.com.smiths@mail.telepac.pt

B&B

Map 1 Entry 4

Quinta da Bouça d'Arques

Rua Abreu Teixeira, Vila de Punhe, 4905-641 Viana do Castelo, Minho

In the grounds of the grand, 300-year-old manor are these modern apartments: the Abreu Teixeira family have lived here for centuries and have combined their talents to create a stylish conversion. Old stone walls, contemporary glass panels and modern art – sheer minimalist chic. Splashes of colour contrast with dark antiques – pink and red striped silk wall-hangings above fine old beds – while neutral colours blend beautifully with beams, tiles, terracotta floors, granite doorways and painted wooden shutters. Hunting prints, baskets, blankets and tall glass vases filled with petals add character, while bathrooms are luxurious with hand-painted tiles, deep baths and fluffy towels. A woollen cushion on a carved bench, a blanket on a sofa, burning inscense, a silk-clad mannequin – all contribute to the serenity of this place. Start the day with breakfast on your own terrace, or in the sitting room with its deep sofas; then move to the wooden loungers by the pool. And there are courtyards and vineyards to explore. A deeply relaxing place with surprising touches at every turn.

rooms	5 apartments: 4 for 2, 1 for 4. 7 cottages: 6 for 2, 1 for 4.
price	€595-€1,120 per week.
meals	Self-catering with breakfast provided. Restaurant 8km.
closed	Never.
directions	A28 Porto-Viana junc. 21 on N103 Braga-Barcelos. At r'bout N13 for Viana do Castelo. After 4km right N308 for Vila Verde & Baroselas. At blue sign for house, left, follow cobbled road; on left.

	João & Ana Luisa Magalhães Couto
mobile	+351 968 044992/936 070630
fax	+351 226 154765
email	joaomcouto@net.sapo.pt
web	www.boucadarques.com

Self-catering

Map 1 Entry 5

Quinta de Malta

Lugar da Igreja, Durrães, 4905-070 Barroselas, Minho

The breakfasts alone are worth the trip: sumptuous spreads of breads, fruits, cheeses, walnut cake, cherry jam, served in an airy, barn-like room with views that swoop across the vines. Maria Helena bought and extravagantly restored this *turismo de habitacão* ten years ago and has made it her life... she makes lace, keeps goats, ducks, chickens and pampers her guests. You arrive down a sloping cobbled drive shaded by vines and there is the quinta — immaculate, vast. It has a lovely position on the side of a hill, there's the distant toot-toot of the train and the church bells ring every quarter hour. Inside, large floor areas are divided into four apartments with a total of ten bedrooms. You get sitting rooms, games rooms and simple kitchenettes, heaps of luxury and a sauna by the pool. The classy bedrooms have elegant repro beds, polished wooden ceilings and sweeping parquet; the fabulous big bathrooms are stocked with towels. If you prefer to properly self-cater, the Adega, once used for wine-making, has become a smart apartment for six. Quite a place!

rooms	10 + 1: 5 doubles, 4 twins, 1 suite (can be rented as 4 apartments). Apartment for 6.
price	€85. Self-catering prices on request.
meals	Dinner, 3 courses, from €25.
closed	Rarely.
directions	IC29 Porto/Viana, exit 11 for N13. At r'bout turn for Viana do Castelo, 4km, right towards Barroselas. Pass Barroselas; sign on right to Durrães, then Quinta. Keep right to top of village; on left.

	Senhora Maria Helena Sobreiro
tel	+351 258 773773
fax	+351 258 778668
email	reservas@quintademalta.com
web	www.quintademalta.com

B&B & Self-catering

Map 1 Entry 6

Casa de Arrabalde

Arcozelo, 4990 Ponte de Lima, Minho

Cross the Roman footbridge straight into town from this elegant, walled manor house on a lively street. The young couple who run it are great fun, enjoy meeting people and manage to juggle busy careers with family life; she is passionate about Portuguese literature, he is studying for his Doctorate in economics and they both teach. There's a pretty music room with a fabulous stucco ceiling, a well-stocked library, and the reception rooms are serenely relaxing. Big, old-fashioned, TV-free bedrooms are furnished with carved antiques, red scatter rugs, Chinese pottery. For privacy you may prefer one of the self-catering apartments in the peaceful grounds next to the pool; they have functional interiors with simple new Portuguese furniture, good views to the hills and are ideal for families. The laid-back Casa is a convenient spot from which to explore the area – but book early: they get busy during the festivals. The market, held every other Monday, is a treat, with villagers from all over gathering to sell their wares.

rooms	3 + 2: 1 double, 2 twins. 2 apartments for 4.
price	€80. Singles €76. Apartment €130.
meals	Restaurants within walking distance.
closed	Rarely.
directions	Cross bridge towards Lima. At roundabout, 1st right (Transito local); right after 50m. House on left after 300m.

Doutor Francisco Maia e Castro

tel	+351 258 742442
mobile	+351 962 518609
fax	+351 258 742516
web	www.casadoarrabalde.com

B&B & Self-catering

Map 1 Entry 7

Casa de Pomarchão

Arcozelo, 4990-068 Ponte de Lima, Minho

Casa de Pomarchão goes all the way back to the 15th century but owes its present look to a rebuild of 1775 when a baroque chapel and veranda were added. The noble old manor house stands at the centre of a 60-hectare estate of vineyards and thick pine forest. Your choice is between the apartment in the main building (every inch the aristocrat's domicile) and one of the seven equally charming outbuildings, perhaps the old stables or the olive press. Some are classical in style (Milho and Bica), others have a more rustic feel (Toca and Mato). What they share is deep comfort and traditional good taste: top-quality sofas, warm curtains, old prints, good beds, original fireplaces, well-equipped kitchens. Homemade cakes and jams are brought over for breakfast; French windows open to your garden or terrace. Stroll the estate, swim in the old irrigation *tanque*, walk to Ponte de Lima, plan a day at the beach. This is such a fine place run by such charming people you could easily stay a week. Frederico's wife greets you with a warm smile, and speaks very good English.

rooms	Apartment for 2; 7 houses for 2-4.
price	€65-€70 for 2. €115-€130 for 4.
meals	Self-catering. Restaurants a short walk.
closed	10-30 December.
directions	2km outside Ponte de Lima on N201 to Valença. Signed.

Senhor Frederico Villar

tel	+351 258 741742
fax	+351 258 742742
email	frederico-vilar@clix.pt
web	www.casadepomarchao.com

Self-catering

Map 1 Entry 8

Casa da Várzea

Várzea, Beiral do Lima, 4990-545 Ponte de Lima, Minho

You'll see Casa da Várzea as you wind your way up from the valley below.
It would be hard not to fall in love with the beauty of the place, cradled among
terraced vineyards. It lay abandoned for many years, but Inácio Caldas da Costa,
who was born here, took courage and after his retirement set about the
restoration of the family seat. Várzea now has six big, light and charmingly
decorated rooms. Family antiques are here for you to enjoy; you may find
yourself in grandmother's or great-uncle's bed, made in cherry. Prints and
framed embroidery, polished wooden floors and rugs are endearingly domestic.
And in the public rooms wood-clad floors and ceilings lend warmth to grandeur
– there's a lovely old chest with a secret drawer for hiding gold sovereigns. At
breakfast there are long views from the airy dining room, plus homemade jams
and fruit from the farm. There's a library, a pool-with-a-view and the old wooden
'drying house', now a second sitting/playroom – and a bar for tasting local vinho
verde. Above all, Inácio and his wife will give you a genuine welcome.

rooms	6 + 1: 2 doubles, 2 twins, 2 family rooms. 1 apartment for 4.	
price	€70. Singles €60. Apartment €100.	
meals	Occasional dinner €20.	
closed	Rarely.	
directions	From Porto-Valença m'way at Viana do Castelo, towards Ponte da Barca for 6km to S. Martinho Gandra. Right to Beiral for 2km, church on left; 200m, on left.	

	Senhor Inácio Barreto Caldas da Costa
tel	+351 258 948603
mobile	+351 964 464389
email	casa.da.varzea@sapo.pt
web	www.solardavarzea.com

B&B & Self-catering

Map 1 Entry 9

Casa de Dentro 'Capitão-Mor'

Vila-Ruivães, C.180, 4850-341 Vieira do Minho, Minho

This was the home of Capitão-Mor de Ruivães who put the French to rout during the Peninsular War (the 'War of Independence' to the Portuguese). It sits proudly on one side of the valley that divides the Cabeira and Gerês mountain ranges, in the tiniest of hamlets amid terraced vineyards and deep greenery. Both hosts and home exude warmth and welcome. Ilda, a retired school teacher, relishes sharing her knowledge of this corner of the Minho: she has maps ready for your walks and will tell you about the region's fascinating mythology. We loved the sitting room with its low beams, granite hearth, old copper still and wall cabinets displaying the family china — just the place for nestling down with a good book. The bedrooms are as unassuming as the rest of Ilda's home; varying in size, they have antique beds and wardrobes, parquet floors, rugs and pretty bedside lamps. Breakfast is as generous as you'd expect: yogurts, homemade jams, fruit juice and Ilda's very special cake, *bola de carne folar*. All this and a tennis court, a pool-with-a-view and the Gerês National Park on your doorstep.

rooms	5 + 1: 4 doubles, 1 twin. Apartment for 6.
price	€63. Singles €50. Apartment €180-€190 (€1,100 per week).
meals	Restaurants in village.
closed	Rarely.
directions	From Braga, EN103 to Ruivães. At sign, Turismo de Habitacão, right. House in centre of village, to right of church.

	Senhora Ilda de Jesus Truta Fraga de Miranda Fernandes
tel	+351 253 658117
mobile	+351 968 466363
email	casadedentro@clix.pt
web	www.casadedentro.com

B&B & Self-catering

Map 1 Entry 10

Pousada do Gerês-Caniçada / S. Bento
Caniçada, 4850-047 Caniçada, Minho

The mountains surround you and the top of the world feels close. These views are hard to beat – watch the sun reflect on the river far below as you sip your sundowner on the terrace. The chalet-style building is not old but looks perfect in this landscape; inside, a peaceful atmosphere prevails. The sitting room, with its high beamed celings and sofas to sink into, is a comfortable spot to curl up with a book, particularly in winter when the fires are lit. The restaurant serves a great selection of mountain dishes, the local cheeses are delicious, as are the Portuguese wines, and there's a cosy bar to retire to. Bedrooms, some small, the best with a balcony, have warm blankets on simple, wooden beds. Bathrooms are white and fresh. Take a dip in a pool that catches the sun all day long, wander the terraced gardens, try your hand at tennis. And there's plenty of fantastic trekking in the protected Peneda-Gerês National Park – friendly, smiling staff will tell you about the best routes. With its breathtaking views, this small hotel is a treat for lovers of the great outdoors.

rooms	28 twins/doubles.
price	€120–€180. Special offers available - see web site.
meals	Dinner, 3 courses, from €30.
closed	Rarely.
directions	From Braga N103 towards Póvoa de Lanhoso & Vieira do Minho. Follow signs to Caniçada. Pousada signed on left.

	Senhor Albino Rolim
tel	+351 253 649150
fax	+351 253 647867
email	recepcao.sbento@pousadas.pt
web	www.pousadas.pt

Hotel

Map 1 Entry 11

Pousada de Amares

Santa Maria do Bouro, Mosteiro Sta. Maria do Bouro, 4720-633 Amares, Minho

A simple village, an austere exterior, a funky hotel. We love this place, with its minimalist interiors, modern art and big spaces – the ancient monastery has been transformed. Architect Eduardo Souto Mouro has turned the colonnaded section of the ruins into the central feature, spring water still flowing through the space; now the ancient irrigation channels run down to a lovely, oval, marble pool, candlelit at night. Light streams in through every corner, some bedrooms have floor to ceiling windows with long views to the Serra de Cabrera, there are pencil sketches, rich hangings – even antique doors – hung decoratively on walls. In the restaurant, vaulted ceilings, a stone chopping table laden with food, and ancient stone bread ovens at the back. A second dining room has a cavernous ceiling and contemporary low-hung chandeliers; people marry here, the speeches flowing from the high prayer balcony above. The old olive and wine room, an elegant spot for conferences, still has the high wooden doors for horses and carriages. Drink in the views, the tranquillity and the simplicity of it all.

rooms	32: 14 doubles, 16 twins, 2 suites.
price	€170-€312. Special offers available - see web site.
meals	Dinner, 3 courses, from €30.
closed	Never.
directions	From Braga N103 for Póvoa de Lanhoso. At Gerez do Minho N205 for Amares. Pousada signed.

Senhor Albino José Rolim Marques

tel	+351 253 371970
fax	+351 253 371976
email	recepcao.bouro@pousadas.pt
web	www.pousadas.pt

Hotel

Map 1 Entry 12

Quinta de São Vicente

Lugar de Portas, Geraz do Minho, 4830-315 Póvoa do Lanhoso, Minho

Dogs dozing in the shade set the pace; a flower-filled oasis, ideal for those who love peace and tranquillity, country walks and birdsong. Teresa and Luís are delightful and will welcome you to their traditional bougainvillea-clad Minho farmhouse. This is an enchanting place: relaxed, solidly comfortable, and unostentatious. An enormous drawing room feels more like a conservatory with high windows opening on two sides, family photos, a woodburner and plenty of sofa space. The dining room is off to one end; at breakfast there will be a big spread and a chance to admire the large collection of old porcelain. In warmer weather you eat out under the orange trees with views of surrounding hills and the farm's kiwi fruit vines. Bedrooms are manicured, large and filled with unusual antiques. Cor de Rosa has its own veranda, Amerelo is perfect for families, Azul is rather smaller, but pretty. Ask to be shown the unusual paintings in the Quinta's chapel (1623) and find time to visit the diminutive castle of nearby Póvoa do Lanhoso.

rooms	3 + 1: 3 twins/doubles. House for 2-4.
price	€70. House €95-€140.
meals	Dinner with wine, €18, by arrangement. Restaurants a short drive.
closed	Rarely.
directions	From Porto A3 north. Exit Braga Sul & Celeiros. Follow Braga Sul, Chaves & Póvoa de Lanhose (N103). Left for Amaraes; after 2km left for Turismo Rural. Signed.

	Senhora Teresa V Ferreira
tel	+351 253 632466
fax	+351 253 635377
email	info@quintasaovicente.com
web	www.quintasaovicente.com

B&B & Self-catering

Map 1 Entry 13

Casa de Requeixo
Frades, 4830-216 Póvoa do Lanhoso, Minho

At about the time that Columbus was discovering America, the Casa was coming into the possession of Ana's family: 1498 to be precise. Looking out onto wooded hills and surrounded by farmland, this once stately home is now a wonderful place for families. Manager Luis is an agricultural engineer, teaches in cooperative agricolas, promotes organic methods and co-runs a small vegetable garden with the village school. It is he who brings breakfast to you on the mezzanine balcony, and there's a kitchen where you can make your own meals. Bedrooms, furnished with faded family pieces, embody the relaxed and easy-going ambience of the farm, while the one-bedroom apartments have their own diminutive terraces, kitchenettes and living rooms with old stone 'sewing' seats — *namoreiras* — set into the windows. In the old cowshed, Luis keeps seven horses and organises rides to the castle in Póvoa do Lanhoso for a brush with medieval architecture. Naturally, all manure is recycled and guests are encouraged to get their hands dirty! Few frills, but great value for money, and wonderfully relaxing.

rooms	4 + 2: 2 doubles, 2 twins. 2 apartments for 2-4.
price	€50. Apartments €455 per week.
meals	Guest kitchen. Restaurant within walking distance.
closed	Never.
directions	From Braga, 16km along N103 towards Chaves. Ignore turning for Póvoa de Lanhoso, follow sign for Frades. House in centre of village.

SPECIAL GREEN ENTRY see page 16

B&B & Self-catering

	Senhor Luis de Matos e Silva
tel	+351 253 636591
mobile	+351 968 021478
fax	+351 253 636499
email	casaderequeixo@sapo.pt

Map 1 Entry 14

Casa Moinho da Porta

Casa de Campo, Taide, 4830-755 Póvoa do Lanhoso, Minho

It's a bumpy ride down the deeply wooded valley to reach this casa, isolated yet close to Póvoa de Lanhoso whose teetering castle dominates the landscape. The stream flows all year round and there's even a waterfall to complete the heavenly backdrop. In a stunning conversion from corn mill to cottage, the old machinery has been respectfully exposed, while wood and stone blend in with stylish modernity and a snazzy open stair. Natural fabrics combine with modern art in light and spacious bedrooms, where views of woods are easy on the eye. During the day, the choice is whether to idle away the hours on the shaded lawn or cool off in the pool and drip-dry on the decking. Pretty tiles don't detract from the practical nature of your kitchen: the mill's new engine room. An English couple staying at the time of reviewing waxed lyrical about the privacy and peace. Close by is a studio, to be rented separately or jointly. Reluctantly you will venture out, perhaps tempted by the prospect of mouthwatering wild boar served at the top of the hill. *Minimum stay two nights at weekends. Unsuitable for small children.*

rooms	Mill cottage for 4. Studio for 2.
price	€980-€1,435 per week.
meals	Self-catering. Restaurants 3-4km.
closed	Rarely.
directions	From Braga, N103 dir. Chaves. 10km, right to Póvoa do Lanhoso; then N 205 Cabeceiras/Fafe. 4km, right to Taíde (Igreja)/Bobeiro. After 1.5km, fork right to Igreja; pass graveyard on right; 700m dirt track, then right; on for 600m.

	Maria João Amaral & José Augusto Vieira
mobile	+351 937 082822
fax	+351 253576577
email	info@casamoinhodaporta.com
web	www.casamoinhodaporta.com

Self-catering

Map 1 Entry 15

Casa dos Lagos

Estrada de Bom Jesus 71-73, 4710-261 Braga, Minho

A calm, dignified welcome awaits you. The house was built by a viscount at the end of the 18th century on a wooded hillside which it shares with the Bom Jesus sanctuary; don't miss the extraordinary baroque staircase that zigzags up to the chapel, and visit on a weekday to avoid the crowds of pilgrims. Both the devout and the less so are welcome at Andrelina's home – a lesson in quiet elegance. Light floods in through the French windows of the sitting/dining room; at one end hangs a fine chandelier under which there will be cake for breakfast, at the other, a velvet sofa draws up to a large fireplace where you may sip a pre-dinner glass of port served from a decanter. The terrace gives onto a garden where stands of camellia break up the order of carefully clipped box hedges and ornamental fountains; the views from here are breathtaking. Only one bedroom is in the main house. It is large, elegantly corniced and has a fine antique furniture: a marble-topped dresser, a cavernous wardrobe, an ornately carved bed. Other rooms and the apartments are more modern, and are large and well-equipped.

rooms	3 + 4: 3 twins/doubles. 4 apartments.
price	€80. Singles €69. Apartment for 2, €80; for 4, €130.
meals	Restaurants 2km.
closed	Rarely.
directions	From Braga, EN103 to Bom Jesus. House is signed on left.

Senhora Andrelina Pinto Barbosa

tel	+351 253 676738
fax	+351 253 679207
email	casadoslagosbomjesus@oninet.pt
web	www.casadoslagosbomjesus.com

B&B & Self-catering

Map 1 Entry 16

Quinta da Pindella

Rua de Pindela, Vila Nova de Famalicão, 4770-130 Cruz, Braga, Minho

Though you're close to Porto, it's blissfully quiet here. The 80-hectare organic farm is in a wide and beautiful valley and has been in the family for 600 years. The cottages are hidden well away from each other, and from the lovely 15th-century house, where Alexandra and Gonçalo live with their parents. (Arrange to dine there in the medieval kitchen.) Soutelo, the largest, is 17th-century, solid and traditional – a typical Minho dwelling. Built of honey-coloured stone and facing south, it has big comfortable bedrooms with separate bathrooms and a well-equipped kitchen with masses of space. The long wooden veranda looks down over woods and fields; behind is a pool set in the lawn. Bouça, once the farm manager's house, is contemporary, elegant, truly charming; Pastor, homely and compact, is just behind the Quinta, so you are more in touch with the farm. Whichever you choose, you will be looked after by a delightful bunch of young people in love with nature, eager that you should enjoy life on their farm. You can explore on horseback, too, with Gonçalo or Francisco. *Minimum stay one week in summer.*

rooms	3 cottages: 2 for 4, 1 for 6.
price	€75-€160.
meals	Self-catering.
	Dinner, with wine, €25.
closed	Rarely.
directions	Leave the A3 at Cruz. Left onto N14, right at traffic lights, round cemetary, left down Rua do Vale, keep right into valley.

	Alexandra Machado & M. Jose Pereira
mobile	+351 914 691987
	+351 919 062100
email	pindela@sapo.pt
web	pindella.tripod.com

SPECIAL
GREEN ENTRY
see page 16

Self-catering

Map 1 Entry 17

Quinta do Convento da Franqueira
Carvalhal CC 301, 4755-104 Barcelos, Minho

The 16th-century monastery is hidden away among cork oaks, eucalyptus, cypress and pine trees. The cloister is thought to have been built with stones from the ruins of the castle of Faria. Certainly the brothers came here for the splendid isolation and the spring which now feeds a pool, built above ornamental steps and with excellent views of house and church. Five centuries on, the granite buildings have been restored to their former grace by the Gallie family, a labour of love for 'how things were'; the results are delightful. Rooms are generously proportioned and have fine antiques, both English and Portuguese. There's a four-poster in one room, old prints, pretty bedside lamps and stuccoed ceilings. The snug, simple courtyard apartment is a fun hideaway with a roll-top entrance and terrace with gentle views. The estate produces its own vinho verde from vineyards that roll right up to Franqueira's walls; ask to be shown the winery. Children have swings in the gardens and a rocking horse in the play room. Be sure to visit Barcelos market. *Minimum stay two nights.*

rooms	4 + 2: 2 doubles, 2 twins. 2 apts: 1 for 2; 1 for 2 + child.
price	€100-€105. Singles €75. Apartments €560-€630 per week.
meals	Restaurant 4km.
closed	November–April.
directions	A11 exit 3 Barcelos; left lane Viana do Csto. 2nd right Póvoa de Varzim. Right under bridge, 2nd left to Franqueira. Through village; middle road of 3 up hill into woods to bar. Right, follow sign; left after church.

	Piers & Kate Gallie
tel	+351 253 831606
fax	+351 253 832231
email	piers@quintadafranqueira.com
web	www.quintadafranqueira.com

B&B & Self-catering

Map 1 Entry 18

Pousada de Guimarães - Santa Marinha

Costa, 4810-011 Guimarães - Santa Marinha, Minho

The peaceful presence of the Augustinian monks lingers and the place is bathed in music – gentle chants in the open courtyard, Bach's melodies rolling around the lofty dining room… their echoes in the old chapter hall stir the soul. Dona Afalda, wife of the first king of Portugal, gave the building to the church and it watches over the town in which Portugal was born. The original features of the monastery remain – its decorative façade, its ancient *azuelos* – yet a captivating modern hotel has evolved. Outside, plenty to explore – a lake, a fomal garden, a trickling stream and grotto. The new pool is set apart and has a bar, there's a huge square for aperitifs. Wide corridors lead to small double bedrooms made up of former monks' cells; you get great views from key-hole windows and bathrooms that sparkle. For atmosphere we prefer the old building to the new wing; ask for a room with a view of Guimaraes below. An old-fashioned drawing room, modern art, entertainment for children, a fountained terrace, delicious *bacalhão* with corn bread for supper, and breakfast fit for a king.

rooms	51: 20 doubles, 29 twins, 2 suites.
price	€150-€311. Special offers available - see web site.
meals	Dinner, 3 courses, from €30.
closed	Never.
directions	From Porto A3 towards Braga, then A7 Guimarães. In town follow signs for Pousada de Sta. Marinha to top of hill.

	Senhora Maria de Jesus Patrão
tel	+351 253 511249
fax	+351 253 514459
email	recepcao.stamarinha@pousadas.pt
web	www.pousadas.pt

Hotel

Map 1 Entry 19

Quinta de Cima de Eiriz

Lugar de Cima de Eiriz, Calvos, 4810-601 Guimarães, Minho

On a south-facing slope of the beautiful Penha mountain, this old Minho quinta has been completely restored. Marvel at the size of the granite lintels, flagstones and building blocks of the entrance hall; in the beamed and terracotta-tiled guest living room the old grape press has been transformed into an unusual raised bar — help yourself to a drink. The pillar-box red of the doors and windows lends a lighter note. Bedrooms are in the old stable blocks, updated with central heating and phones and sparkling marbled and tiled bathrooms. Most memorable of all are the views over the trimmed lawns and across the valley. Breakfast is a big meal: fresh orange juice, yogurt, several types of bread and cake and homemade jams. Afterwards you can stride straight out towards the wooded summit of Penha. In the warmer months cool off in the pool; there is also an excellent games room. The views are long and rural, and 10km away is ancient Guimarães with its narrow streets, castle and superb museum. Closer still: the Santa Marinha da Costa Monastery, the best preserved medieval building of the region.

rooms	4: 1 double, 3 twins.
price	€65. Singles €50.
meals	Restaurants 5km.
closed	Rarely.
directions	A3 Porto-Braga. In Vila Nova de Famalaicão, A7 to Guimarães; towards Fafe & Felgueiras. After 4km, right for Felgueiras for 4km; right at sign Penha & Lapinha. After 2km, left at stone cross; signed.

	Doutor João Gaspar de Sousa Gomes Alves
tel	+351 253 541750
mobile	+351 966 242174
fax	+351 253 420559

B&B

Map 1 Entry 20

Douro

Residencial Castelo Santa Catarina

Rua Santa Catarina 1347, 4000–457 Porto, Douro

This eye-catching building was built high up above Porto during the period which the Portuguese call the Gothic Revival. Even if the corner turrets and window arches don't remind you of Notre Dame, you can't fail to be intrigued by this tile-clad edifice – it stands like a folly, surrounded by tall swaying palms, in a traditional residential area. The interior décor is as surreal as the exterior. Be regaled by gilt and stucco, chandeliers and mirrors, cherubs and lozenges, Tiffany lamps and roses, repro beds and cavernous wardrobes. It's showy, over the top, faded in parts, garish in others – and great fun. There is ongoing restoration of paintwork and the bathroom tiles are often out of step with the rooms but these things are part of the charm. The delightful João is normally around in reception and with fluent English can answer all your questions about this whimsical building. Book the suite in the tower with views, or a room opening to the flower garden complete with pretty cat. An enormously entertaining city hotel that readers have praised.

rooms	24: 21 twins/doubles, 3 suites.
price	€70. Singles €50. Suite €90.
meals	Restaurants nearby.
closed	Rarely.
directions	At top of Rua Santa Catarina, just below Plaza Marques Pombal. Follow signs.

Senhor João Brás

tel	+351 225 095599
fax	+351 225 506613
email	porto@castelosantacatarina.com.pt
web	www.castelosantacatarina.com.pt

Hotel

Map 1 Entry 21

Pensão Avenida

Avenida dos Aliados, No. 141 4° 5°, 4000-067 Porto, Douro

Smack bang in the centre of Porto, this friendly, inexpensive guesthouse is run by the delightful João Brás and his wife. They also own Castelo de Santa Catarina and go the extra mile to make your stay special. On the fifth floor of a typical 19th-century townhouse, reached by lift, are these very plain, simple, bright and spotlessly clean rooms. Breakfast is a good spread and is served in the light-filled cream breakfast room overlooking the square and the impressive government buildings. The odd antique is dotted around but the feel of this place is relaxed and unpretentious. Do ask for local maps; the S. Bento train and tube station is outside the door, as are excellent restaurants and cafés. Walk to monuments such as Torre dos Clérigos, Sé Cathedral, Palácio da Bolsa, to Ribeira and the famous Oporto cellars – or travel up the river Douro by boat; information is provided at reception. A simple place to lay your head with a great welcome and terrific value for money. *Show your copy of Special Places to Stay and João will let you park free at the Castelo de Santa Catarina hotel nearby.*

rooms	15: 5 doubles, 8 twins, 2 triples.
price	€40-€50. Singles €30.
meals	Restaurants nearby.
closed	Rarely.
directions	Centre of Porto, opposite Town Hall & São Bento station, near Praça de Liberdade.

	Senhor João Brás
tel	+351 222 009551
fax	+351 222 052932
email	pensaoavenida@clix.pt
web	pensaoavenida.planetaclix.pt

Guest house

Map 1 Entry 22

Casa dos Esteios

Quinta do Ameal, 5 Miguel de Paredes, 4575-373 Penafiel, Douro

The granite farm buildings, encircled by kiwi plantations, have been beautifully converted. The wine cellar is now an open-plan living/dining room, the grape press the base for the woodburning stove, the old stables are luxurious bedrooms. No expense has been spared; it is fresh, bright, uncluttered – a happy blend of antique and modern. A stone bread oven rubs shoulders with a sleek, cream, Swedish-style fitted kitchen with granite work tops, where smiling Daniella, who was born here, makes tasty breakfasts. The dining room is deeply traditional with its dark wooden table and English and Portuguese antiques. Wooden floored bedrooms, set around the courtyard, have armchairs and more dark antiques, enlivened by fabrics patterned with English roses and pretty checks. New bathrooms are luxurious and sparkling. The pool has views to the hills and a small play area for children. Make time for the renowed spa town of Termas de São Vicente, and Porto, a short drive. This is a super place for a group of friends to rent, and an easy, relaxing spot for a few days' B&B.

rooms	6: 5 doubles, 1 twin. Whole house available.
price	€70. Singles €55. Whole house €1,600 per week.
meals	Restaurants nearby.
closed	Never.
directions	From Porto IP4 to Penafiel. Exit for Nó de Guilhufe (Penafiel Sul & Entre-os-Rios) on N106 for 12km. Left to Rio de Moinhos on N312; right at sign for Casa dos Esteios.

	Senhora Maria Jorge Nogueira da Rocha
tel	+351 217 591894
mobile	+351 962 830701
fax	+351 217 591894
email	nogueirarocha@netcabo.pt

B&B

Map 1 Entry 23

Pousada do Marão / São Gonçalo

Serra de Marão, Ansiães, 4600-520 Amarante, Douro

The Marão mountain range awaits you, and you can gaze down the valleys from your bed. Smart tartan-dressed beds have headboards with carved hearts, there are balconies, fluffy bathrobes and lashings of hot water – a comfortable and comforting place to come back to after a long day's walk. You can even breakfast on your own terrace. This pousada has a small, intimate feel and friendly local staff. In the lounge is a winter-lodge atmosphere thanks to roaring fires, leather chairs, panelled ceilings, baskets, sisal mats on polished floors and red tartan armchairs. Amarante, the nearest town, is devoted to Saint Gonçalo who, according to legend, was the matchmaker patron saint. The atmosphere is intimate, and romantic – candlelit dinners at individual tables, then an aperitif in that cosy lounge. The exterior is not much to write home about but once inside you will fall under the spell of this dear little hotel. Do visit the Mateus Palace and the art gallery of Amadeo Sousa Cardoso – or just sit back and relish the views.

rooms	15: 6 doubles, 8 twins, 1 suite.
price	€120–€380. Special offers available - see web site.
meals	Dinner, 3 courses, from €30.
closed	Rarely.
directions	IP4 towards Vila Real, junc. 21. Pousada signed.

	Senhor João Amaral
tel	+351 255 460030
fax	+351 255 461353
email	recepcao.sgoncalo@pousadas.pt
web	www.pousadas.pt

Hotel

Map 1 Entry 24

Casal de Aboadela

Aboadela, 4600-500 Amarante, Douro

You'll long remember arriving at Aboadela. Once you turn off the busy main road you twist and turn along the narrowest of lanes to this delightfully sleepy hamlet and its old farmhouse. There is many a treat in the rambling gardens: an old granite maize store, a bubbling spring, gourds and pumpkins drying in the sun, old millstones recalling the building's origins. There are roses and oranges and vines and, in among them, secluded places for contemplation. The bedrooms are in the main house, simply attired in cottage style with family furniture and lacking nothing; just to one side in a converted outbuilding is the 'stone little house' (sic) which is self-contained – with a barbecue – and would be just perfect for a longer stay. The guest sitting/dining room is similarly unpretentious: granite-walled with a tiled floor and potted plants. Home-grown wine is available. A French window gives onto a small balcony and lets in the morning light and the view; your attentive hosts will spoil you at breakfast. There are lovely rambles straight out from the house and the São Gonçalo monastery in Amarante is a short drive.

rooms	4 + 1: 3 twins, 1 suite (1 twin, 1 single). House for 2.
price	€45. Singles €40. Suite €50. House €55.
meals	Picnics & snacks by arrangement. Restaurants 3-10km.
closed	Rarely.
directions	From Amarante, IP4 for Vila Réal. 9km after Amarante, right to Aboadela; follow signs for 'Turísmo Rural'; right at T-junct.; follow 'TR' sign to house.

	José Silva & Helena Rebelo
tel	+351 255 441141
fax	+351 255 441141
email	srebelo@med.up.pt

B&B & Self-catering

Map 1 Entry 25

Casa da Levada

Travanca do Monte, Cx. 715, Bustelo, 4600-530 Amarante, Douro

The crenellated tower is visible as you come down the winding cobbled track into this ancient hilltop village, perched amid mountain views. Levada is really a small castle in a settlement built of rough-hewn, moss-covered granite blocks where people and animals still live cheek-by-jowl. Rough wooden doors open to reveal a goat, a pair of oxen, an old woman embroidering: scenes from centuries past. The house is a mountain refuge, and hosts Maria and Luís are wonderfully welcoming. She is an English teacher, he a humorous man whose family have lived here for 300 years. You'll sleep in bedrooms with granite walls, wooden ceilings, beams and sisal matting. The Tower Room has a separate bathroom across the landing and a balcony; the Poet's Room has a trapdoor down to the bathroom. The sitting room is comfortable and the dining room barn-like, with a large oval table at which everyone eats together: food is traditional and the wine comes from Luís's mother's farm. Up the hill, pass granite water mills to a bleak hilltop with great boulders and dolmens. An amazing place.

rooms	5: 1 double, 3 twins; 1 twin with separate bath.
price	€75-€90. Singles €60-€72.
meals	Dinner, 3 courses with wine, €25. Restaurants 2-15km.
closed	Rarely.
directions	From south A4. After Amarante, exit 18 to Régua & Mesão Frio. Follow for 8km, then right for Turismo d'habitacão. On for 2km to Travanca do Monte, right, house after 600m.

Luís & Maria Vasconcelos do Lago Mota

tel/fax	+351 255 433833
mobile	+351 936 472946
email	casalevada@clix.pt
web	www.casalevada.com

B&B

Map 1 Entry 26

Casal Agrícola de Cevêr
Quinta do Pinheiro, 5030 Santa Marta de Penaguião, Douro

Grapes are still crushed by foot in this winery, on the western reaches of the Douro. Alice and son Filipe opened up their 19th-century house six years ago, while continuing to produce their own-label port and olive oil. All visitors are invited to tour the production areas and to sample the latest offerings. Rooms are comfortable and airy with up-to-the-minute bathrooms; for a small extra charge you can take the suite with its own little gallery. National Trust colour schemes combined with good 19th- and early 20th-century antiques create a mood that is calm and reasonably formal. Guests have their own sitting room with smart striped sofas and walls of books on what to do and see in this most beautiful region. There's a large basement games room with a pool table, too. For warm days there's a Roman swimming pool set on its own lawned terrace, against a backdrop of vines. Dinner in the family dining room is incredible value and includes wine, port and coffee. Very few English people have found their way here – a pity, as they are missing something special.

rooms	5: 3 doubles, 1 twin, 1 suite.
price	€80. Singles €70. Suites €90.
meals	Dinner with wine, 3 courses, €25. By arrangement.
closed	Christmas.
directions	From Porto A4 to Vila Real. Take Santa Marta de Penaguião exit onto N2. House clearly signed on right, just before entering village.

	Filipe Manta & Alice João Mergulhão
tel	+351 254 811274
fax	+351 254 811274
email	casalagricoladecever@casalagricoladecever.com
web	www.casalagricoladecever.com

B&B

Map 1 Entry 27

Casa d'Além

Oliveira, Mesão Frio, 5040-204 Mesão Frio, Douro

The cheerful façade of Casa d'Além looks out across the stunning terraced vineyards of the Douro valley and reflects the optimism of the early 1920s. The public rooms are the most refined: the Rennie Mackintosh print on easy chairs, sofas and drapes is perfectly balanced by the delicate wrought-iron work of the balconies. Piano, card table and shining parquet create an atmosphere of old Portugal. Next door is a panelled dining room and, still more remarkable, a long painted corridor, a 'marbled sunburst', which leads to your bedroom. A feast of period pieces, there are rugs and marble-topped dressers, generous old tubs and wash stands. Rooms have heavenly views. Paulo and his wife speak excellent English and their marvellous staff will take care of you; ask Elisabete about personal trips along the Douro by boat or steam train, and visits to Mateus Palace in Vila Réal. Outside are views, pure air and a secluded pool area. Be sure not to miss dinner: perhaps a roast from their bread oven, homemade ice-cream and a chilled glass of the local wine.

rooms	3: 1 double, 1 twin, 1 family room.
price	€80. Singles €65. Family room €85–€100.
meals	Lunch & dinner, 3 courses, from €20. Light meals €8.
closed	Rarely.
directions	From Porto, A4 for Vila Réal. N108 to Régua. N108 to Régua. After Mesão Frio, on for 8km to Granjão. Under railway bridge, then left to Oliveira. Signed on left.

	Senhor Paulo José F S Dias Pinheiro
tel	+351 254 321991
fax	+351 254 321991
email	casadalem@sapo.pt
web	www.casadalem.pt

B&B

Map 1 Entry 28

Pousada de Mesão Frio

Solar de Rede, Sta. Cristina Estrada Nacional nº108, 5040–336 Mesão Frio, Douro

A grand, palacial *solar* – a country manor – high in the hills, exuding 17th-century elegance and prosperity. It's now a formal hotel, with doormen and butlers and furniture fit for a king. Antique blue and white tiles in the entrance hall show traditional Portuguese scenes; carved high-back chairs, huge flower displays and gold laquered furniture add a touch of decadence. Views from the bedrooms in the main house stretch far east and west along the river Douro, and the steep terraces grow the precious grapes for port. (The hotel makes its own; enjoy the wine tastings, take some home.) Bedrooms have antique furniture and pretty soft furnishings, and the main house suite is a dream. We also like the secluded stone 'cottages' that have been converted into spacious suites. Most have balconies or terraces, all are decorated with floral fabrics giving a cottagey feel. Dine grandly in the old kitchen – or, equally grandly, in the dining room, where parties may gather around one big solid table and drink from silver goblets. A pretty chapel is attached – and the pool overlooks the river.

rooms	29: 21 twins/doubles, 1 suite, 7 cottage suites.
price	€150–€230. Singles €174. Special offers available - see web site.
meals	Dinner, 3 courses, from €30.
closed	Rarely.
directions	N108 to Mesão Frio. Pousada signed on left.

Senhor Joaquim de Sousa

tel	+351 254 890130
fax	+351 254 890139
email	solar.da.rede@douroazul.com
web	www.pousadas.pt

Hotel

Map 1 Entry 29

Casa de Vilarinho de São Romão

Lugar da Capela, Vilarinho de São Romão, 5060-630 Sabrosa, Douro

An old place with a young heart. Here is a fine combination of old and new, of warm sunny colours, light and space. The 17th-century house overlooks the Pinhão valley, and has a much older chapel at its entrance. Cristina gave up teaching art to concentrate on the house, and later she turned her attention to the vineyards – her ancestors, who came to Portugal from Holland, are an established port-wine family. All is harmony and light: white walls, pale floors strewn with kilims and rugs, enormous rooms, grand paintings, fine antiques. The sitting room is huge, cool and contemporary, with matching sofas and plenty of books. One of the bedrooms has twin brass beds and solid granite window seats, another an ornately carved bed. Bathrooms are immaculate, some with walk-in showers. Outside is a shaded terrace where you may breakfast in summer (fresh juice and fruits from the farm), an inner gravelled courtyard with dolphin-spouting fountains and a serene pool. All this, lovely walks along old hunting tracks and, always, those long, long views across the Pinhão valley.

rooms	6: 2 doubles, 4 twins.
price	€85. Singles €70. Extra bed €20.
meals	Dinner €25, by arrangement.
closed	Christmas.
directions	From Vila Real to Pinhão through Sabrosa; in Vilarinho de São Romão, you will see green wood gateway & chapel on left. Through gate.

	Senhora Cristina van Zeller
tel	+351 259 930754
fax	+351 259 939288
email	mail@casadevilarinho.com
web	www.casadevilarinho.com

B&B

Map 1 Entry 30

Casa de Casal de Loivos

Casal de Loivos, 5085-010 Pinhão, Douro

Oh the views! Among the best in this book — or anywhere. This northern manor has been home to the Sampaios since 1733. The house is in the village, yet from the front you see few dwellings — and the mighty Douro far below. It is a marvellous sight and every room opens to it. Tradition, comfort and gentility are the hallmarks here. Manuel is a truly old-fashioned, charming gentleman, and attracts a cultivated clientele; he speaks perfect English, usually sports a cravat and likes you to dress for dinner. Traditional meat and fish dishes are created from old family recipes, and are always excellent. The dining room is simply beautiful, and dominated by its white-clothed table; dinner conversation should be stimulating. There's a comfortable sitting room that opens onto the breakfast terrace, then it's down to the pool. The view-filled bedrooms are gorgeous, elegantly furnished with good bathrooms. Fuelled by good food and wine, bewitched by the interplay of light, land and water, and pampered by Manuel and his courteous staff, you'll feel halfway between earth and heaven.

rooms	6: 3 doubles, 3 twins.
price	€95. Singles €70.
meals	Dinner €22.50, by arrangement.
closed	1–25 December; January.
directions	From Pinhão to Alijó; 1st right & up through vineyards until Casal de Loivos. House on right at end of village.

Senhor Manuel Bernardo de Sampaio

tel	+351 254 732149
fax	+351 254 732149
email	casadecasaldeloivos@ip.pt
web	www.casadecasaldeloivos.com

B&B

Map 2 Entry 31

Casa do Visconde de Chanceleiros

Largo da Fonte, Chanceleiros-Covas do Douro, 5085-201 Pinhão, Douro

The lap of Douro luxury with hosts whose aim is to make you wish you need never leave. Welcome to a world of big comfortable beds, squashy armchairs, lovely bathrooms, thick fluffy towels, great views, space inside and out, and friendly hosts and dogs. Kurt and Ursula's home is a classic granite and white manor house on the edge of a hillside village, with vine-covered terraces on one side. Wide granite steps lead down to the terrace where there is a huge pool with a long-roofed cabana furnished with sofa, stereo and tables. There are wrought-iron sunbeds with plump cushions, a sauna in a port barrel and an outdoor jacuzzi. All is tasteful and stylish, informal yet not over-casual. Indoors, lots of strong, warm colours set off by terracotta, slate and granite, and a mix of antique and modern furniture. The large colour-themed bedrooms are like big bedsitting rooms (one on two floors, ideal for a family) and have beautiful hand-painted furniture and beds. Breakfasts are feasts, and don't miss the splendid three-course dinners. All this and masses to do: ping-pong, tennis, squash, billiards, boules...

rooms	9: 8 suites, 1 family room.
price	€95-€120. Singles €95.
meals	Lunch €20. Dinner with wine €30, by arrangement.
closed	Rarely.
directions	IP4 from Porto to Vila Real; exit for Chaves. At r'bout follow signs to Sabrosa. There, turn for Pinhão. There, follow signs for Chanceleiros.

	Kurt & Ursula Böcking
tel	+351 254 730190
fax	+351 254 730199
email	chanceleiros@chanceleiros.com
web	www.chanceleiros.com

Guest house

Map 2 Entry 32

Quinta do Passadouro
Vale de Mendiz, 5085-101 Pinhão, Douro

It's a typical port-wine quinta, perfectly positioned above a small river, imbued with that homely yet stylish decorative touch that comes so naturally to the Dutch. Ronald and Jet have been here five years and leave the wine-making to the Portuguese. Ronald, ex-wine trade, organises walking and wine tours, Jet cooks, and dinners are sociable and great fun. (You may even find yourself joining in with the washing up!). Your hosts live in the next village but return to prepare a fine breakfast before you've stirred from your pillow. Bedrooms are an appealing blend of modern and old, with big beds, huge wardrobes, modern paintings and pleasing colours; shower rooms are compact and in good order. Views stretch over the valley to the vines beyond and through the olive and juniper trees you can glimpse the river below. Bliss to laze in a deckchair on the lawn, dine on the terrace, or catch the train at Pinhao for a trip along the Douro. The whole place is exceptionally peaceful, wonderfully relaxing and great value for money. *Five self-catering dwellings for four in Trás-os-Montes, €545-€745 per week.*

rooms	6: 4 doubles, 2 twins. Whole house available.
price	€62.50. Whole house from €330 per day.
meals	Dinner with wine & port, €26.50. Picnic available.
closed	Rarely.
directions	From N322 Pinhão-Alijó, turn for Vale de Mendiz, signed Quinta do Passadouro. After village, house on right.

	Ronald Weustink & Jet Spanjersberg
tel/fax	+351 254 731246
mobile	+351 938 136067
email	quintadopassadouro@oninet.pt
web	www.quinta-do-passadouro.com

B&B & Self-catering

Map 2 Entry 33

Casa da Azenha
Rio Bom - Portelo de Cambres, 5100-421 Lamego, Douro

Even if it's raining and you're hovering with your maid beneath the umbrella, you may still notice the coat-of-arms caught between plinth and terracotta. Senhor Manuel Mascarenhas Gaivão is the notary in Régua, a distinguished gentleman who summons all the trappings of nobility to this side of the river. This is *turismo de habitaçao* in the grandest style, so expect formal luncheons with uniformed attendants, finger bowls between courses, cultured conversation with Senhora Gaivão, and afternoon strolls around the pool and perfumed gardens. Encased by the lovely Douro valley and terraces steeped in vine, the house was built by Manuel's ancestors and you'll notice the recurring family motif on bedspreads and curtains. Bedrooms in the house are elegant and antique, two opening to the gardens, all with flowing curtains and collections of china. The diminutive self-catering apartment has a kitchenette that makes room for an attractive blue and gold sitting area. Your brush with Portugal's silver spoon does present hardships however — mealtimes will never be the same again. *Minimum stay two nights.*

rooms	5 + 1: 2 doubles, 2 twins, 1 single. Apartment for 2-4.
price	€95. Single €85. Apartment €125 (€875 per week).
meals	Lunch & dinner with wine, €30.
closed	Christmas.
directions	A24 exit for Régua. Cross River Douro south, direction Resende. Follow signs to house.

Manuel Mascarenhas & Ana Maria Gaivão

tel	+351 254 666205
fax	+351 254 667019
email	info@casa-azenha.com
web	www.casa-azenha.com

B&B & Self-catering

Map 1 Entry 34

Quinta da Timpeira
Penude, 5100-718 Lamego, Douro

A cool, calm home close to the Sanctuary of Nossa Senhora dos Remédios, where pilgrims still climb the 700 steps on their knees. The immaculate, post-war house clings to the hillside and is bordered by a topiaried box hedge; below are terraces, pool, tennis court and orchard – space for alfresco lunch. Opposite are the Meadas mountains, behind are the vineyards that supply the nearby Raposeira sparkling wine factory. The house is comfortable in an uncluttered way and manageress Senhora Édite looks after you warmly. Bedrooms are not particularly roomy but are excellently decorated with a mix of old and new. Two on the lower floor share a bathroom and are next to a sitting room with games – good for families. Bathrooms are smart. The split-level sitting/dining room is striking with its long curved wall and spectacular views from its vast window and balcony. Dinner at the crisply laid table is traditional Portuguese, accompanied by Timpeira wines. There's a small 'shop' downstairs where you can buy local handicrafts, and a bar, a wine cellar and a ballroom!

rooms	7: 4 doubles, 3 twins.
price	€70-€75. Singles €57-€60. Suite €120.
meals	Lunch/dinner with wine €22.50, by arrangement.
closed	Rarely.
directions	From Lamego N2 for Viseu. Quinta da Timpeira is 2.5km after Raposeira sparkling wine factory, on left.

Senhor José Francisco Gomes Parente
tel	+351 254 612811
fax	+351 254 615176
email	quintadatimpeira@gmail.com
web	www.quintadatimpeira.com

B&B

Map 1 Entry 35

Trás-os-montes

Casa das Cardosas

Rua Central, Folhadela, 5000-103 Vila Real, Trás-os-Montes

A grand Trás-os-Montes manor in as bucolic a setting as you could hope to find – yet you are a mile from Vila Real. The Cardosa family has been here for 250 years and once made wine. The glorious gardens produce peaches, plums, cherries and raspberries, and there's a pool. Find time to let the warm-natured Maria Teresa tell you a little of the area's history over a chilled drink on one of her three terraces (what views!). Bedrooms are a step back in time, darkish but quiet, elegantly decorated without a hint of hotel. One has an ornate Bilros four-poster, the 'French' room has pretty fabrics and a chandelier, the back room, the smallest, leads enticingly to the terrace. The old stone dormitory for grape pickers has become a roomy winter sitting room with rugs on shining parquet, innumerable antiques, fresh flowers and family mementos – all add up to a mood of unaffected intimacy. Breakfast at Cardosas is a generous meal with homemade jams, juices and eggs; at dinner you may feast on roast beef, or hake from the wood-fired oven. Make sure you have time to explore the Alvão Natural Park.

rooms	3: 2 doubles, 1 twin.
price	€60. Singles €55.
meals	Lunch & dinner by arrangement.
closed	Rarely.
directions	In Vila Réal head to university. Turn right to village; signs to the house begin at the left of the main entrance to the university.

Senhora Maria Teresa Cardosa Barata Lima
tel	+351 259 331487
mobile	+351 962 929750
fax	+351 259 331487

B&B

Map 1 Entry 36

Casa Cabrilho

5470-019 Lapela-Cabril, Trás-os-Montes

Lively, engaging António is determined to put this mountain hamlet on the culinary map. He and his father make a great team: António trained as a cook in Australia and London; dad, once a waiter on a cruise ship, tends the picturesquely sloped vegetable garden. You'll get more than rice and chips here; the restaurant serves fresh vegetables, home-smoked ham, local *cabrito* (kid) and hearty soups and stews. Small bedrooms play second fiddle: just cork floors, floral covers, bare ceiling bulbs, a shared bathroom, an extra wc. (Note the balustrade-free steps up the rooms and the sheer-drop terrace: leave the toddlers at home!) It's hardly a place for lovers of luxury, but it's perfect for those in search of the 'real' Portugal. Hikers wanting to spend a night in this remote landscape would be as happy as anything, while the village's stony charm is being nurtured. Spend the day in the hills of the Peneda-Gêres National Park, than back for a dip in the pool, a game of billiards and a splendid supper. A no-frills, peaceful place to stay, simply miles from the beaten tourist track. *Free guided walk for groups of eight.*

rooms	4 doubles sharing bathroom (let to same party only).
price	€40. Singles €30.
meals	Lunch & dinner €15.
closed	Rarely.
directions	From Braga, EN103. After Ruivães, turn off for Cabril & Ponte da Misarela; 15km to Lapela.

	Senhor António Goncalves
tel	+351 253 659260
email	res.cabrilho@sapo.pt

Map 1 Entry 37

Quinta da Mata
Estrada de Valpaços, Nantes - AP. 194, 5400-581 Chaves, Trás-os-Montes

Filinto found this 17th-century house, restored it beautifully, and opened up to guests. The food is a treat: for breakfast, miniature pasties, homemade bread, Chaves ham, smoked sausage; for dinner, served at a table for 12, a hearty *cozido* (stew) perhaps, and a good wine from Valpaços. Quinta da Mata's bedrooms are equally special. The chestnut floors, dark panelled ceilings, dressed stone walls and hand-painted tiles are the perfect backdrop for Arraiolos rugs, crocheted bedcovers and well-chosen antiques; cut flowers and the lingering scent of woodsmoke add yet more character. For space choose one of the suites, big enough to lounge all day in; one has a library/office, the other a whirlpool bath. In the well-tended gardens are two tennis courts (Filinto is a qualified coach) and a pool, there are bikes to borrow and peaceful walks through the thickly wooded slopes of the Brunheiro mountains. Filinto's charm is infectious and our inspector has happy memories of afternoon tea with him at a table groaning under cheese, jam, doughnuts and cake. *Light aircraft flights available.*

rooms	6: 2 doubles, 2 twins, 2 suites.
price	€80. Singles €69. Suites €100.
meals	Dinner, with wine, €18.
closed	Rarely.
directions	Just outside Chaves; N213 to Valpaços, through Nantes; signed.

Senhor Filinto Moura Morais

tel	+351 276 340030
mobile	+351 919 448035
fax	+351 276 340038
email	quintadamata@mail.telepac.pt
web	www.quintadamata.net

B&B

Map 2 Entry 38

Pousada de Bragança

São Bartolomeu, Estrada do Turismo, 5300–271 Bragança, Trás-os-Montes

White and functional outside; confident, contemporary and luminous within.
The Pousada has bags of style and views that sweep over the walled city of
Braganca and to the hazy Trás-os-Montes mountains… you could spend all day
on your pretty balcony watching the sun travel across the scene – and set.
Below is an elegant pool; beyond, across the river Ferrenga, the towers of the
remarkable 12th-century citadel. Rooms are sleekly modern with pale wooden
floors and panelling, clean-cut furniture, creamy rugs and colourful bedspreads,
bathrooms are smart in pink granite. The same polished mood is reflected in the
main rooms of the hotel where plate-glass windows make the most of the light.
And everywhere, bold splashes of modern art – paintings, ceramics, sculptures,
tapestries. Staff are friendly, efficient and full of suggestions for day trips and
walking or cycling routes in the nearby Montesinho Natural Park. Popular with
families – there's a children's pool – and couples, the hotel has a relaxed yet lively
atmosphere. Bragança is lovely – a 25-minute walk downhill, a taxi ride back.

rooms	28: 5 doubles, 23 twins.
price	€120–€180. Special offers available - see web site.
meals	Dinner, 3 courses, from €30.
closed	Never.
directions	From Porto, IP4 to Vila Real, then continue to Braganca. There, follow signs.

	Senhor João Amaral
tel	+351 273 331493
fax	+351 273 323453
email	recepcao.sbartolomeu@pousadas.pt
web	www.pousadas.pt

Hotel

Map 2 Entry 39

La Hoja de Roble

c/Costanilla 13, 49300 Puebla de Sanabria, Zamora, Spain

Thirty minutes over the border, in Spain, the ancient town on its isolated promontory is stunning. And just down from its 15th-century castle is this 17th-century Castillian inn. Young entrepreneur Gustavo spends most of his time in the cellar-bar tempting visitors with the local red, Toro… or Albariño or Rioja — a delightful preamble to a meal in a beautifully dressed restaurant: perhaps a plate of 'habones' (butter beans) and juicy beef from Sanabria. Or octopus, a local speciality — an exciting choice for a land-locked region. The nobleman who owned this house 300 years ago left behind furniture and complete sets of linen and china, stored on the ground floor where they have always been. Minimalist-rustic bedrooms are charming with local-linen curtains, intricately carved beds, chunky stone walls, reclaimed beams and subtle use of colour; some have balconies from which you may look down on the bustling street below. After a day wandering the serene shoreline of the Lago de Sanabria, bliss to return to a deep bath in a mosaic'd bathroom. Worth the detour.

rooms	6 twins/doubles.
price	€60-€90. VAT included.
meals	Breakfast €6. Lunch & dinner €20-€25. VAT included.
closed	1-15 February; 4-20 November.
directions	From Orense/Madrid on A-52; exit 79 for Puebla de Sanabria. Cross river Tera and immediately turn left at T-junc. into town centre. After 300m, at fountain square, hotel on right beside kiosk.

	Senhor Gustavo Alonso
tel	+34 980 620190
email	info@lahojaderoble.com
web	www.lahojaderoble.com

Guest house

Map 2 Entry 40

Beira

Photo Casa dos Matos, entry 63

Casa da Cisterna

Rua da Cadela, 7, 6440-031 Castelo Rodrigo, Beira

Tucked beneath the ruined Castelo Rodrigo, reached by cobbled streets lined with artisan shops, is a delightful casa. Next to the village's water-trapping cisterna, it can be entered on one level of the hillside and exited by another. The local authority has been handing out grants to encourage residents to restore these properties, which explains the cohesion of warm earthy tones and ancient stones. Birdwatchers will feel comfortably at home in stylishly contemporary bedroom eyries – two in a converted outbuilding – whose namesakes 'Pisco' (robin) and 'Andorinho' (swift) fly past the windows making Spain an effortless glide away. Everyone sits around the dining room table for ambrosial hilltop breakfasts including fresh yogurt and honey, before climbing the stairs to a sitting room that opens elegantly to wooden decking and a sloping lawn. Ana is your young and informal host, an ornithologist who makes stimulating conversation. She divides her time between looking after you and, alongside her husband, raising a very rare local breed of donkey.

rooms	4: 2 doubles, 1 twin, 1 suite.
price	€65-€100.
meals	Picnic €15 p.p. Restaurants in village.
closed	Rarely.
directions	Leave Guarda on A25; exit 32 for Almeida; follow signs for Figueira Castelo Rodrigo. Right for Castelo Rodrigo; at r'bout at entrance to village, right, then left.

	Ana Berliner
tel	+351 271 313515
mobile	+351 917 618122
email	casadacisterna@casadacisterna.com
web	www.casadacisterna.com

B&B

Map 2 Entry 41

Casa Campo das Bizarras

Rua da Capela 76, Fareja, 3600-271 Castro Daire, Beira

Drive through the apple orchard to the fine old granite farmhouse where a corner of old Portugal has been lovingly preserved. Cool in summer, the house has bags of rustic character with heavy oak beams, stone floors and a cobbled wine cellar. There's a delightful reading room and an upstairs drawing room crammed with family treasures and mementos of farming life. The long, low kitchen has a large inglenook fireplace, bread oven and a marble-topped table for breakfast: try the homemade cheese and compotes; ask about nearby excursions. There are two bedrooms in the main house and three in an adjoining wing. Dark antique furniture contrasts with creamy curtains, many edged with the regional lace. All have private bathrooms (some just across the corridor), with delicate Art Nouveau tiled mirrors. Apartments are in a cluster of farm buildings and have basic cooking facilities but there's also a communal kitchen, and a barbecue. The pretty raised pool has Roman steps and terracotta tiles. Jacó, a human-sounding parrot, and the elderly donkeys in the garden amuse visiting children.

rooms	5 + 5: 5 twins/doubles, some with separate baths. 4 apts: 3 for 2-4, 1 for 2-5.
price	€50-€64. Singles €38-€50. Apts €72-€109 (€700-€850 per week).
meals	Lunch & dinner by arrangement. Restaurant 20-minute walk.
closed	November.
directions	From Castro Daire to Fareja. In Fareja left at sign for Turismo Rural. Past church, up narrow cobbled lane, Bizarras on right.

	Senhora Marina Rodrigues Moutinho
tel	+351 232 386107
fax	+351 232 382044
email	casa@campodasbizarras.com
web	www.campodasbizarras.com

B&B & Self-catering

Map 1 Entry 42

Casa de Cela

Cela, Urrô, 4540-645 Arouca, Beira

Captain Correlli comes to Portugal. Picture a scene where chickens and ducks waddle through the outdoor dining area and into the organic vegetable garden: utterly rural. Retired doctor José Carlos does not stand on ceremony; this used to be his practice after all, and the house has been in the family since 1754. The grown-up children all help out, most of all Cláudia, who divides her time between managing the property and teaching eco-tourism. Everything has been sensitively adapted, the character richly retained in chestnut wood ceilings and doors that bring warmth to enormous, chandeliered rooms, while huge new bathrooms are replenished daily with fresh flowers on marble washstands. More countrified rooms in the new annexe open onto Art Nouveau verandas replete with old *massieras* (dough bins). Breakfast is served in the *saliero* where the hams were once salted under the arches; now the tables are loaded with Cláudia's pumpkin jam. Homemade raspberry ice-cream by the pool is hard to resist, or one of the cooling salads from a menu as green as the garden grows.

rooms	9: 4 doubles, 1 twin. Annexe: 4 twins.
price	€82-€90.
meals	Lunch up to €17.50. Dinner €18.
closed	Rarely.
directions	From IC2/N1 Oliveira de Azemeis to Vale de Cambra towards Arouca. Just past Cela village sign; house on left.

	Senhora Cláudia Pina Rebelo
mobile	+351 919 445818
fax	+351 256 944226
email	casadecela@gmail.com
web	www.casadecela.com

Guest house

Map 1 Entry 43

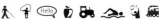

Casa das Ribas

Lugar do Castelo, 4520-220 Santa Maria da Feira, Beira

The 'house of the steep banks' is perched on a hill with views to the Atlantic; the charming cobbled old town lies below. The 16th-century house with 'new' 1820 wing was originally a religious foundation; enter another age. In the entrance hall, a family coat of arms: this B&B is a stately home. There are several drawing rooms, polished parquet, chandeliers, religious icons, flagged kitchen with vast inglenook and a preponderance of dark wood. The atmosphere, however, is easy, and Dona Maria Carmina is the most solicitous, family-welcoming hostess; nothing is too much trouble. Bedrooms are relatively simple after the profusion of downstairs – fresh and spotlessly clean, with fine beds, firm mattresses and up-to-date bathrooms. The large, L-shaped Bishop's Room has seven shuttered windows, while the more rustic Casa do Caseiro, in the delightful grounds, makes a special holiday cottage. Maria has the greenest fingers; there's a box-hedged courtyard and masses of untamed space for children. And there are a library, a *sala da musica* with grand piano, a games room and a beautiful 16th-century chapel.

rooms	6 + 1: 5 twins/doubles, 1 suite. House for 4-6.
price	€60-€75. Singles €50. Suite €75. House €100.
meals	Restaurants nearby.
closed	Rarely.
directions	Exit Lisboa & Porto m'way at Feira & follow signs for Castelo; you can see castle in trees on way into Feira; house next to castle.

Senhora Maria Carmina Vaz de Oliveira
tel   +351 256 373485
mobile   +351 962 770705
fax   +351 256 374481

B&B & Self-catering

Map 1 Entry 44

Pousada da Murtosa-Torreira/Ria

Torreira – Pico de Muranzel, 3870-301 Murtosa-Torreira, Beira

You could be at the end of the world. Perched on the skinny isthmus that separates the Atlantic from the lagoon of the Aveiro, the road ends just south of the pousada. Overlooking the water and backed by dunes, it has a dreamy setting that is perfect for anyone seeking walks, birdlife or the simple play of light on water. It is a 1960s building of a low-rise, open-plan design, its acreage of glass making the most of those mesmerising watery views. Reception rooms are cool and airy with slate floors and pale colours while bedrooms have a breezy New England beach-house flavour: cream painted furniture, marine blue fabrics, crisp tiled bathrooms. Stand on your balcony and watch the fish gliding through the lagoon below. The waters are unsuitable for swimming but you can watch, or join, the fishermen in their bright, gondola-style *moliceiros*. Take a dip in the pool and watch the sun rise over the dunes; hire a bike and cycle to São Jacinto, at the end of the isthmus, for Atlantic sunsets. Return to supper: shellfish, grilled bream, or, if you dare, eel stew.

rooms	19 twins/doubles.
price	€120–€240. Special offers available - see web site.
meals	Dinner, 3 courses, from €30.
closed	Never.
directions	From Lisbon IP1 north. At junc. 17 follow signs for Murtosa on N109. Continue over river; south on N327 for Torreira. Pass town & continue south; signed.

	Senhor Pedro Pinto
tel	+351 234 860180
fax	+351 234 838333
email	recepcao.ria@pousadas.pt
web	www.pousadas.pt

Hotel

Map 1 Entry 45

Quinta da Vila Francelina

Vila Francelina Frossos, Albergaria-a-Velha, 3850-663 Aveiro, Beira

Tall and stately, this gleaming 19th-century house splashed with Art Nouveau tiling hangs above the Rio Vonga. Views sweep from the pool across the extraordinary bird- and willow-strewn *pateira* (water meadow) that spreads into the Aveira lagoon, 17 kilometres down the coast. This dreamy landscape is reflected in the gracious house, where walls and ceilings are hand-painted with beautiful scenes of gardens, rivers and wildlife. António and Mariá have spent three years restoring their home; high and airy bedrooms are elegant and comfortable with grand polished bedheads, tall windows, Art Nouveau touches. Choose the top-floor room under the eaves for its tiny veranda and inspirational views. By contrast, the low stone annexe is sharp and modern, a hint of chic urbanity: bold paintings on white walls, rugs on polished floors, sleek lighting and superb bathrooms. And there's plenty of space here to unwind: in the library, the games room (table tennis, snooker) or on the court. Walk in the pine and eucalyptus forest or take a boat trip through the dreamy water meadows.

rooms	10: 3 doubles. Annexe: 7 doubles.
price	€85. Singles €75.
meals	Lunch & dinner €25. Kitchens on request.
closed	Rarely.
directions	A1 Aveiro norte/Viseu exit towards Aveiro. Take exit for Angeja/Cacia and left in Frossos/S.João de Loure. Quinta 2km on.

António & Mariá Pinho

mobile	+351 917 203471
fax	+351 234 934942
email	info@quintadavilafrancelina.pt
web	www.quintadavilafrancelina.pt

Guest house

Map 1 Entry 46

Casa de Sol Nascente

Rua de Alagoa, Taipa, Requeixo, 3800-881 Aveiro, Beira

East meets west in 'the house of the rising sun'. The architecture is the work of Ian's Japanese wife Chizu, whose paintings hang in many rooms (and in the Tokyo National Gallery). Enter to a column of glass around which curves a flight of stairs; light pours in. More curved walls, and graduated shadows, to "bring nature into the living room and soften the mood." Soothing downstairs bedrooms contain an immaculate blend of pieces from around the world, along with satellite TV; the suite on the upper floor has a glamorous bathroom, and a terrace. Chizu and Ian are welcoming and well-travelled, as easy with city slickers as with young families; the mood is gentle and relaxed. Meals from Chizu are superb and span a wide range of Portuguese and Japanese cooking; in the summer there are wonderful barbecues under the bamboo pergola, resplendent with vines and kiwi fruit, and a large lush garden. Breakfasts are mighty, snacks are on request. Nearby are the gorgeous Aveiro lagoons, full of birdlife, and sandy beaches are five miles away. Ian is a qualified meditation instructor: ask about weekend retreats.

rooms	4 + 1 : 2 doubles/twins, 2 suites. Apartment for 6.
price	€45. Suite €78. Apartment €930 per week.
meals	Lunch & dinner by arrangement.
closed	Rarely.
directions	A1; EN235 for Aveiro; immed. right to Mamodeiro; at 1st café, 1st junc. right to Requeixo. On to Taipa. Road bends down to right; at bend take smaller road going up on right; last house, 800m.

	Ian & Chizu Arbuckle
tel	+351 234 933597
fax	+351 234 933598
email	arbuckle@mail.telepac.pt
web	www.solnascente.aveiro.co.pt

B&B & Self-catering

Map 1 Entry 47

Quinta de Baixo

Rua. Quinta de Baixo, 3510-014 Viseu, Beira

Buried in a deeply wooded valley, yet within walking distance of Viseu's historic centre, the Quinta still has a rural feel. Sadly, the house was ruined in the revolution; during its modernisation, the family lived in what is now a self-catering annexe, which will appeal to aficionados of Seventies' style. The Dutch family live in the Quinta; Carolina, a delightful and enterprising young woman, manages the house and lives next door, with her pony and partner. As the morning light creeps into the dining room, buttery croissants glisten in the sunshine and breakfast becomes a time to bask. The pace has then been set for a gentle amble through the delicious 'French' garden, before braving the untamed woodland of the lower valley. After a full day's exploration and dinner in Viseu, relax in traditional Portuguese bedrooms that display high ceilings and tall doors, draped windows, antique beds and dark parquet floors. Families will appreciate the more private rooms upstairs, and the games room under the sloping attic roof. A thoroughly welcoming and homely place.

rooms	5 + 1: 3 doubles; 2 doubles with separate bathrooms. Apartment for 6.
price	€80. Apartment €500-€700 per week.
meals	Restaurants within walking distance.
closed	Rarely.
directions	Leave IP3 (r'bout Paulo VI); continue to A24. At next r'bout, go back the way you came & take 1st right. Then right; left to house.

Ronald Weustink & Jet Spanjersberg

tel	+351 232 421035
mobile	+351 965 869190
fax	+351 232 421739
email	info@quintadebaixo.com
web	www.quintadebaixo.com

Quinta do Rio Dão

3440-464 Santa Comba Dão, Beira

Perfect for lovers of the great outdoors – the setting is a dream. The house hides
in a stand of old oaks on the banks of the small lagoon. Dutch owners Pieter
and Juliette live here with their two boys – bought up on the farmstead when it
stood in ruins – and have sensitively restored it in traditional Beira style. They are
excellent, multi-lingual hosts, and give you the choice of B&B in their house or
self-catering apartments and cottages. A traditional Portuguese look marries with
a clean, uncluttered approach to space, and there's nothing too showy to detract
from the natural beauty of the place. Bedrooms are not large but have a sunny
feel; bathrooms are modern, there are lots of verandas and captivating views
down to the river. In summer, life is spent mostly outdoors; birdsong at breakfast,
and, at night, the lights of Santa Comba Dão twinkling across the water. With
canoes, a rowing boat and a windsurfer for guests to borrow, this would be an
idyllic place for a sporting holiday. Almost the feel of a mini holiday village – and
great value. *Minimum stay two nights.*

rooms	4 + 5: 4 twins/doubles.
	2 apartments for 2-4;
	3 cottages for 4-8.
price	€55-€65. Apartments €55-€65.
	Cottages €100-€195.
meals	Restaurants 5-10km.
closed	Rarely.
directions	From Lisbon, A1 for Porto. After
	Coimbra, IP3 for Viseu. 500m before
	Santa Comba Dão turn to Vimieiro.
	Follow sign Agro Turismo for 4.5km
	to Quinta.

	Pieter & Juliette Gruppelaar-Spierings
tel	+351 232 892784
fax	+351 232 892372
email	quinta2@quintadoriodao.com
web	www.quintadoriodao.com

B&B & Self-catering

Map 1 Entry 49

Pousada de Vila Pouca da Beira

Convento do Desagravo, Calçada do Convento, 3400-758 Vila Pouca da Beira, Beira

The Convento do Desagravo was built on the orders of the bishop and a count, Dom Francisco de Faria Pereira, during the last quarter of the 18th century. It is a beautiful building, with a fine bell tower and dozens of arches. The result of a first-class restoration is a peacefully stylish hotel. Hallways have creamy walls, earth-coloured cushions, stone floors and wrought-iron furniture; the central courtyard, flanked by stone pillars, has a natural pool in its centre. In the living rooms are bold red sofas on terracotta-tiled floors, local furniture and antique pieces from the convent, including some stunning carved gilt work, now hung artistically on the walls. Generous bedrooms use neutral and bold colours to effect, with red and cream bedspreads and red and gold latticed headboards. The views are magnificent from the vast bedroom terraces at the back: the Serra da Estrela unfolds before your eyes. The restaurant is formal and serves the best local produce, and there's a pleasant bar, too. After dinner, meander down the vineyard path to the pool and soak up in the peace.

rooms	24: 8 doubles, 12 twins, 4 suites.
price	€150–€230. Special offers available – see web site.
meals	Dinner, 3 courses, from €30.
closed	Rarely.
directions	From Coimbra, IC3 for Penacova, then IC6 to Vendas de Galises. Follow signs for Vila Pouca de Beira; signed, but easy to miss.

Senhora Maria de Jesus Patrão

tel	+351 238 670080
fax	+351 238 670081
email	recepcao.desagravo@pousadas.pt
web	www.pousadas.pt

Hotel

Map 1 Entry 50

Casa da Calle

3400-487 Nogueira do Cravo, Beira

Built in 1743 of the local granite, this handsome house has been in the Tinoco family ever since. Its rooms tell the history – there are collections of everything from books and portraits to decanters and vine scissors. The effect is not remotely museum-like, partly because of the light that floods in through the generous windows and partly because of the warm personality of your hostess. Bedrooms are traditionally furnished with antique beds and wardrobes. Two have splendid *maceira* ceilings. All are given a modern edge with fresh sprigged curtains and covers; new bathrooms have sparkling white tiles. When we visited, Isobel was thoughtfully distributing chocolate and biscuits (as well as a bar list) to the rooms. There are two comfortable sitting rooms – or head out to the camellia lawn where barbecues are served on summer evenings under the weeping pines. Close to the mountains of the Serra da Estrela, you are in wonderful walking and riding country – try a guided horse trek. Three beautiful horses are kept for visitors' use and equipment is available – what a spot to explore!

rooms	3 twins.
price	€60. Singles €40.
meals	Restaurant 3km.
closed	Christmas.
directions	A1 from Lisbon; IC6 & N17 towards Oliveira do Hospital. Left at traffic lights in Vendas de Galizes following signs to Nogueira. House on left exit of r'bout.

	Senhora Isabel Tinoco
tel	+351 238 604878
mobile	+351 914 540768
email	info@casadacalle.com
web	www.casadacalle.com

B&B

Map 1 Entry 51

Quinta das Mestras

Nogueira do Cravo, 3400-430 Oliveira do Hospital, Beira

A bird-dipped stream runs between the rambling stone buildings of the quinta and the cabanas. The old farmstead in its hillocky seven acres is surrounded by pine forests and olive groves; the Serra da Estrela rises nobly beyond. Dutch-born Rob and Australian Leondra – he a designer and cartoonist, she a translator – are engaging hosts whose B&B is as vibrant as they are. Bedrooms are named after the colour of each of their slopey wooden ceilings: Green, Yellow, Pink. Green is perhaps the nicest, with its own terracotta bathroom and ochre-painted wrought-iron beds. Pancakes, omlettes, fruit – something different for breakfast each day is served on suitably rustic plates on a shady terrace, or in the kitchen whose fascinating clutter reflects a lifetime of travel. Up on the hill, sharing a bathroom, are two self-catering cabanas – simple and private. You are two miles from the charming little town of Oliveira do Hospital, river canoeing and swimming are not much further, and fabulous walks start from the door. A fun, wacky place to stay in one of Portugal's prettiest green corners.

rooms	3 + 2: 2 doubles, 1 twin. 2 cabanas.
price	€32.50-€47.50. Cabana €30 (€200 per week). Use of kitchen €10.
meals	Breakfast €5 (for B&B only). Dinner by arrangement.
closed	Rarely.
directions	From Coimbra to Guarda; N17 direction Oliveira do Hospital; just before, exit for N. do Cravo. Between Nogueira & Bobadela. Just off road, signed (blue mailbox).

	Leondra Wesdorp
tel	+351 238 602988
fax	+351 238 602989
email	info@quintadasmestras.com
web	www.quintadasmestras.com

B&B & Self-catering

Map 1 Entry 52

Quinta da Moenda

Avenida da Fronteira, Alvoco das Várzeas, 3400-301 Oliveira do Hospital, Beira

Life is unhurried here. Donkeys pull carts, sheep wander through villages and the bakery is the most important place in town. Tucked between the Açor and Estrela mountains, above the river Alvoco, the quinta has a timeless feel that Hans and Josephine have done little to disturb. The 18th-century water mill and olive mill make up their home. The distillery is converted into apartments, compact and unfussy, with modern pine furniture, terracotta floors and splashes of colour from sofabeds and curtains. A wood-burning stove adds cosiness while the first-floor apartments have flower-potted verandas and mountain views. This is an outside sort of place with walks through pine and eucalyptus forests, hikes onto the tops (in winter, there's skiing in the Serra da Estrela National Park), canoeing or swimming in the river. And there's a lovely riverside walk to the village and the chance of spotting otters. Come back to cool off in the pool or under the pergola; in the evening, raise your glass to the stars with only the rush of the river to disturb the silence. There's a large communal living space, too. *Under 4s free.*

rooms	5 apartments for 2-4.
price	€65 for 2. Extra bed €12.50. Under 4s free.
meals	Self-catering. Restaurant 10-minute walk.
closed	Rarely.
directions	From Coimbra N17 towards Oliveira do Hospital. At Venda da Galizes, EN230 towards Covilhã until Ponte das Trés Entradas. Left on bridge towards Alvoco das Várzeas. 4 km on; house signed on right.

	Josephine van Bennekom & Hans de Herder
tel	+351 238 666443
mobile	+351 961 337611
email	joha@sapo.pt
web	www.quintamoenda.com

Hotel rural Quinta da Geía
Aldeia das Dez, 3400-214 Oliveira do Hospital, Beira

Aldeia das Dez in the foothills of the Serra da Estrela is an old hamlet to which
the 21st century seems only to have given a passing glance. From the outside
you'd never guess that the house is several hundred years old: Dutch owners
Frenkel and Fir have completely renovated the place. Life centres on the lively,
relaxed bar and restaurant – stained wooden tables and chairs, bright tablecloths,
paintings by local artists – and is well frequented by the local folk who obviously
approve of the cooking: traditional Portuguese food with Italian/French slant.
Eat on the terrrace and enjoy the dreamy views of the mountains and tree-filled
landscape. Large, bright bedrooms are attractively finished: pine floors, stone
walls, interesting angles, neutral colours; a suite or apartment would be perfect
for families. Your hosts have mapped out the best walks in the area – follow
Roman pathways through forests of oak and chestnut; the two dalmations might
join you. An excellent place, now with two large conference rooms. *Minimum stay
in apartments three nights; one week in summer.*

rooms	11 + 4: 11 twins, doubles & suites. 4 apartments for 2-6.
price	€65-€85. Singles €55-€75. Suite €90-€100. Apts €100-€125 (€600-€775 per week).
meals	Lunch & dinner from €22.
closed	2-22 January.
directions	From Coimbra, IP3 to intersection with IC6. 4km before Oliveira, at Vendas de Galizes, right signed 'Hotel Rural'; 14km on.

	Fir Tiebout
tel	+351 238 670010
fax	+351 238 670019
email	quintadageia@mail.telepac.pt
web	www.quintadageia.com

Hotel

Map 1 Entry 54

Pousada de Manteigas

São Lourenço, Penhas Douradas, 6260-200 Manteigas, Beira

Built in 1948 — the highest of the pousadas — it has the character of a mountain lodge, with plenty of wood about the place and open fires. Pinch yourself to check you're still in Portugal as you encounter a gift shop selling wintry fur capes and leather hats. You are in the heart of the Serra da Estrela Natural Park and the seasons are clearly defined. Smallish, slightly spartan bedrooms have stout, county-style wooden furniture with cream wool rugs scattered over dark stained floors; curtains and covers are in jolly red and green tartans. The cosy communal rooms offer snooker, chess and somewhere comfy to read a book; it's the sort of place where guests get chatting after a rigorous day's walking, fishing or skiing. The mountain community take huge pride in their pousada and it is perhaps the only one with a song written about it — ask at reception and they may play it for you. Staff will also arrange picnics for walkers and, for the more adventurous, trips to the glacial valley of the Zezere. Try the famous Serra, the local soft cheese — it's delicious.

rooms	21: 11 doubles, 7 twins, 3 family rooms.
price	€150-€180. Special offers available - see web site.
meals	Dinner, 3 courses, €30.
closed	Never.
directions	Lisbon A1 to Torres Novas then A23. Exit Couilha Sul; at Mata Mouros, straight on, close to Teixoto, right onto N232, past Verdelhos, continue to Manteigas. Pousada 13km above town. Signed.

	Senhora Maria José Garcez
tel	+351 275 980050
fax	+351 275 982453
email	recepcao.slourenco@pousadas.pt
web	www.pousadas.pt

Hotel

Map 1 Entry 55

Pousada de Belmonte

Convento de Belmonte, Serra da Esperança, Apt. 76, 6250–000 Belmonte, Beira

The founding fathers of the medieval monastery chose themselves a remote rocky hillside with open views across the plain; now rows of hazelnut trees and olives lead the eye to the pine- and eucalyptus-clad peaks of the Serra da Estrela. The ruins of the original *convento* have been cleverly incorporated into a modern hotel, offering 21st-century comfort and an ecclesiastical flavour. The main lounge occupies the original chapel with a galleried sitting area replacing the choir. The small cloister has been rebuilt as a sheltered place to sit or stroll. Two modern bedroom wings flank the old core – not particularly beautiful on the outside but extremely stylish within. A neutral palette has been adopted, with notes of ochre and terracotta. Rooms are all different, some with elegant wrought-iron light fittings or unusual wooden chairs. The honeymoon suite has an over-sized modern four-poster and its own rooftop terrace for romantic breakfasts. Outside, in a sheltered corner, is a small pool with Atlantic-blue tiles. In town is the family home and last resting place of Pedro Cabral, discoverer of Brazil.

rooms	24: 4 doubles, 19 twins, 1 suite.
price	€170–€311. Special offers available - see web site.
meals	Dinner, 3 courses, from €30.
closed	Never.
directions	From Lisbon A1 to Torres Novas; A23 towards Guarda. Exit for Belmonte & folllow signs for Pousada.

Senhor José Pedro Florindo

tel	+351 275 910300
fax	+351 275 912060
email	pousadadebelmonte@mail.telepac.pt
web	www.pousadas.pt

Hotel

Map 2 Entry 56

Casa do Castelo Novo

Rua Nossa Senhora das Graças - 7, 6230-160 Castelo Novo, Beira

The garden is simple, flourishing, the views are wonderful and the whole place is, according to one reader, "a joy." The Casa is a 17th-century home on the slopes of the Serra da Gardunha, an amphitheatre that drops to the impossibly narrow streets of a hilltop village. The granite front of this elegant casa is deceptive: you cannot guess how the house is built up the steep rock, nor that the garden is at the level of the first floor. The ground floor is a sitting room for guests, with sofas, a wall of rock, carpets from Morocco. Up a wooden staircase to the main living room; more sofas, a granite fireplace, a Maceira ceiling, bookcases cut into the walls, clay figures, modern lithographs, fine china. Feast-like breakfasts are served in a Victorian-parlour style dining room; bedrooms gleam. In the tower: a double and a suite with Dona Maria beds, the latter with the best view in the house. A few steps across the garden and you have a choice of a painted Alentejan double or a romantic twin. Alice and Manuel are very friendly and welcoming and prepare truly delicious Portuguese food.

rooms	4: 3 twins/doubles, 1 suite.
price	€60. Singles €45. Suite €70.
meals	Lunch & dinner, with wine, €20-€25. By arrangement.
closed	Rarely.
directions	A23 to Fundão. 10km south of Fundão, signs to Castelo Novo. Enter on R. de São Brás; at Largo da Bica right along R. da Gardunha, around castle, till R. Nossa Senhora das Graças; signed. Parking is away from house.

Senhora Alice Aleixo

tel	+351 275 561373
fax	+351 275 561373
email	castelo.novo@gmail.com
web	www.castelonovo.web.pt

B&B

Map 4 Entry 57

Quinta das Lágrimas

Santa Clara, Apart. 5053, 3041-901 Coimbra, Beira

Quinta das Lagrimas has a place among the most remarkable hostelries in Portugal. The Palace is 300 years old but was rebuilt after a fire a century ago. Wellington stayed here and was captivated by the place and the legend that the *lágrimas* of the name were those shed by Dona Inês when put to the dagger by the knights of King Alfonso. Come to see ten acres of wonderful gardens – some of which have been taken up by the golf school; species have been brought from all over the world. The elegance of the double sweep of staircase leading to the main front is mirrored within. The dining room is stuccoed, panelled and chandeliered; dignitaries are international but the food is Portuguese and accompanied by fine wines from Lágrimas's large cellars. Bedrooms are fit for kings (a number have stayed here); ask for one in the old house, elegant and deeply luxurious with rich fabrics, vast beds and marbled bathrooms. The new building has minimalist rooms in neutral colours, a restaurant with a modern twist and a spa – the couples' massage the ultimate treat.

rooms	54: 5 doubles, 9 twins, 4 suites. Annexe: 14 doubles, 1 suite for 3. Garden rooms: 21 twins.
price	€149-€210. Singles €119-€173. Suites €339-€410.
meals	Lunch & dinner €48-€120.
closed	Rarely.
directions	A1 to Coimbra; exit for Coimbra south. Head to city centre; signs for Portugal dos Pequenitos on left; Quinta signed.

	Senhor Mario Morais
tel	+351 239 802380
fax	+351 239 441695
email	geral@quintadaslagrimas.pt
web	www.quintadaslagrimas.pt

Hotel

Map 3 Entry 58

Casa Pombal
Rua das Flores 18, 3000-442 Coimbra, Beira

Pombal is the Portuguese for dovecote and this old townhouse is delightful. In Coimbra's narrow streets, on a hill close to the famous seat of learning, it is friendly, utterly unpretentious and will stir feelings of nostalgia for those student years. Four of the rooms have breathtaking views over the old city roofscape and down to the Mondego river. They are basic, comfortable and clean; three have their own bathrooms, but sacrifice a little luxury for the pleasure of those views. A relaxed atmosphere is created by the friendly Dutch owners, who know the town well. Single folk will especially enjoy this place, where you may meet fellow travellers over a leisurely breakfast (eggs, cereals, fresh juices, homemade jams) or relaxing in the small courtyard. Pets are allowed in bedrooms but not the common room or patio. Built on hills overlooking the river, Coimbra is a city to explore slowly; once capital of the (young) nation, it is most famous for its ancient university. Try to visit in term time when students add life to the city and so try to catch Coimbra's male vocalists sing Fado.

rooms	9: 1 double, 3 twins; 1 double, 2 twins, sharing bath; 1 double, 1 twin sharing bath.
price	€40-€58. Singles €28-€48.
meals	Dinner €17.50 (minimum six).
closed	Rarely.
directions	In Coimbra, signs for 'centro' then 'Universidad' via Ave. Sá da Bandeira then towards Praça da Republica; onto Rua Padre António Vieira. Park at end of street. If lost ask for Rua da Matemática.

Anja Ligtenbarg
tel +351 239 835175
fax +351 239 821548
email info@casapombal.com
web www.casapombal.com

B&B

Map 3 Entry 59

Casa da Azenha Velha

Caceira de Cima, 3080 Figueira da Foz, Beira

Once an *azenha* – a flour mill – this large house is now much more: the decorative flourishes above doors and the large rooms suggest a grand history. After Maria de Lourdes and her dog have met you, you will find that the grounds teem with other creatures: deer, ostriches, cows, horses and peacocks. Bedrooms surround a pretty garden and flowers grow up around your windows; they are huge with large wooden beds and pretty coordinating bedcovers, flowers and tiles. Pamper yourself with a soak in the sunken bath – heaven. You breakfast in the large kitchen of the main house; rail-sleepers support the roof bricks, and farming equipment decorates the walls. A sitting room in the old stable block has an honesty bar, comfy sofas, open fire and board games. There are also a pool, a tennis court, a snooker table and a barbecue; experienced riders may borrow a horse. A short walk from the main house is the new, rustic-style Azenha restaurant where you eat regional and international dishes. A perfect spot for families, couples or groups, and great in winter and summer. Excellent value.

rooms	6 + 1 : 2 doubles, 4 twins. Apartment for 2-4.
price	€75-€100. Singles €65. Apartment €115.
meals	Dinner from €10. Restaurant closed Mondays.
closed	Rarely.
directions	From Coimbra, N111 for Figueira da Foz. Shortly before Figuiera turn for Caceira; immed. left following signs Turismo Rural. After 2km right for 500m; right again. House on left.

Senhora Maria de Lourdes Nogueira

tel	+351 233 425041
fax	+351 233 429704
web	

B&B & Self-catering

Map 3 Entry 60

Challet Fonte Nova

Rua da Fonte Nova P.O.Box 82, 2460-046 Alcobaça, Beira

Fabulous ceilings, elegant damask curtains at French windows, classical beds, glass chandeliers, antique dressers – what bedrooms! Equally delightful are the lofty stucco ceilings of the entrance hall, the oriental rugs, the stuffed red ottomans, the green and red couches and the Venetian-style chandeliers. This 19th-century chalet-style house is close to town yet peaceful – and a two-minute stroll from the Alcabaça Monastery World Heritage Site. In recent years a modern annexe has been sensitively added. These newer bedrooms are crisply and elegantly attired, one with a vast marble bathroom. Maria João lives nearby with her young family and is a kind hostess. The overall feel is one of turn-of-the-century graciousness and charm, you almost feel you are on a stage set – great fun. The garden has some formal terracing and beds brimming with agapanthus in summer; indoors are a bar and a snooker room. The hotel is a perfect launch pad for Batalha, another World Heritage Site, and the sweet little fishing village of Nazaré.

rooms	10: 8 doubles, 2 singles.
price	€110. Singles €85.
meals	Occasional meals by arrangment. Restaurant 200m.
closed	24 December–1 January.
directions	200m from Alcobaça Monastery. Head towards the city 'Caldas da Rainha', 1st road on right.

Senhora Maria do Carmo e Adão Lameiras

tel	+351 262 598300
fax	+351 262 598430
email	mail@challetfontenova.pt
web	www.challetfontenova.pt

Hotel

Map 3 Entry 61

Hotel Residencial Casa do Outeiro

Largo Carvalho do Outeiro 4, 2440-128 Batalha, Beira

This small modern guest house is right in the centre of Batalha, its hillside perch ensuring that some bedrooms have views across the town's rooftops to the colossal Abbey. The Abbey was built in gratitude for Dom João's victory over the Castilian army in 1385 and is a masterpiece of Portuguese Manueline art, its exterior all carved pinnacles, columns and buttresses; the innards, especially the cloisters, are exceptionally beautiful too. If you come to visit the Abbey do stay at Casa do Outeiro even if at first appearance it is a rather unexciting place. Bedrooms are roomy and functional; all have modern pine furniture and own baths but their private terraces lift them into the 'special' league, while the wooden floors and ceilings add warmth. Most of the area to the rear of the building is given over to the swimming pool; there's also a snooker room. Ever-helpful Odete will look after you with kindness and will advise you where to dine out and, in the morning, treat you to a generous breakfast that includes five or six homemade jams. Great value.

rooms	15: 10 doubles, 5 family rooms.
price	€43–€65. Singles €40–€50. Family rooms €60–€80.
meals	Restaurants 50m.
closed	Rarely.
directions	In Batalha, follow signs for centre. Hotel signed.

Senhor José Victor Pereira Madeira

tel	+351 244 765806
fax	+351 244 768892
email	geral@casadoouteiro.com
web	www.casadoouteiro.com

Hotel

Map 3 Entry 62

Casa dos Matos

Rua Dom Fuas Roupinho, 2480-032 Alvados, Beira

Here, on the edge of a village in the Serras de Aire National Park, you can explore caves where dinosaurs left footprints. Completely rebuilt from a small village house, Casa dos Matos now reveals clean stone lines and smoothly unfolding terracotta. The sitting room has emerged from the old threshing floor, its essence retained in sections of the original wall – still visible. Massive timbers in a diagonal truss offer a warm frame for an uncluttered scene of large windows, red sofas and woodburners. The modern art that hangs in each funky bedroom suite has been chosen to match the colours, enhancing a minimalist sophistication. It's a place to come to now, before the young and exuberant couple who run it so charmingly exhaust themselves working full-time: Rita as a teacher of landscape management, Rui as forestry engineer. They love company, and organise special courses for their guests, such as birdwatching and mushrooming. All the food is freshly sourced and a local lady supplies wonderful herb teas – best sipped on the veranda as you contemplate the mountains before dinner.

rooms	6 doubles.
price	€70-€80.
meals	Lunch snacks available. Dinner €18.
closed	Rarely.
directions	From A1, exit Torres Novas & follow direction Minde; continue until Alvados; signs for Casa dos Matos.

	Rui & Rita Anastácio
tel	+351 244 440393
mobile	+351 967 601607
email	geral@casadosmatos.com
web	www.casadosmatos.com

B&B

Map 3 Entry 63

Albergue do Bonjardim
Nesperal, 6100-460 Sertã, Beira

Countryside laps up to this elegant 18th-century country house, approached along minute lanes flanked by vineyards and groves of orange, olive and almond. If you enjoy wine you should book at least a night here; the Lenders have a well-stocked cellar and there is a cosy bar for tastings of the estate's organic wine. The bedrooms are big and light, with pine floors, high ceilings, antique beds and dressers and carefully chosen fabrics and colours. Some are in the main house and reached via a fine old granite staircase, others are in an outbuilding and, if booked together, can be joined to make an apartment for six; these have a south-facing veranda and there is a woodburning stove and the same light and uncluttered feel. The pool is indoors, along with a sauna and a Turkish bath. There are also a children's playground, ponies and horses to ride, canoeing nearby and walks galore; but find time to visit the winery with Dutch Hubertus. He is a convivial host and runs courses which cover all aspects of wine. "An oasis of peace," wrote one guest; "a gateway to tranquillity," said another.

rooms	7: 5 twins/doubles, 2 family rooms for 3.
price	€80. Extra bed €21.
meals	Lunch €10. Dinner €25.
closed	Rarely.
directions	From Coimbra, IC8 towards Castelo Branco and exit to Sertã. There N238 towards Tomar. At sign marking beginning of village of Cernache do Bonjardim, left at sign 'Nesperal-turismo rural'. Follow signs.

	Hubertus Johannes Lenders
tel/fax	+351 274 809647
mobile	+351 969 080788
email	albergbonjardim@mail.telepac.pt
web	www.albergue-do-bonjardim.com

Guest house

Map 4 Entry 64

Beira

Casa Lido
Monte da Portelinha, Silveira, 6030-021 Fratel, Beira

This charming cluster of Beira cottages is on the edge of a village frozen in time, directly opposite the village fountain and communal bread oven. Your hosts live in a restored olive mill nearby, and their design talents are reflected in these lovely cottages, all of which keep their traditional wooden ceilings and roughly-rendered white walls. At the heart of the house for six is a magnificent chestnut table and chairs; there are two roof terraces and a galleried bedroom in the old fruit loft. Another roof terrace in the house for four, and furniture fashioned to the owners' design. The cottage has a spiral-iron staircase, a wood-burning stove and views over soft countryside towards the river from courtyard and terrace; the barn is flooded with light and its terrace filled with flowers. Shared by all is a delightful courtyard pool reminiscent of a Roman bath. Charming Lise and Udo will tell you all you need to know, from when the baker drops by to the best restaurants in town. They also run occasional gourmet food weeks and art courses. Special. *Minimum stay three nights.*

rooms	4 houses: 2 for 2, 1 for 4, 1 for 6-8.
price	From €200 per house per week.
meals	Self-catering. Restaurants 4km.
closed	Rarely.
directions	IP2-A23, exit 16 signed Riscada-Juncal; under dual carriageway; left at T-junc. for Silveira. Pass/turn to Riscada and carry on under tunnel to Silveira. In village, follow road round to right; Casa at end.

	Lise & Udo Reppin
tel	+351 272 566393
mobile	+351 914 111469
email	lidoreppin@hotmail.com
web	www.ruralretreatrentalportugal.com

Self-catering

Map 4 Entry 65

Estremadura

Casa da Padeira

EN8 - S. Vicente 19, Alcobaça, 2460-711 Aljubarrota, Estremadura

This no-frills guest house is not old but the bedrooms on the first floor have an antique style thanks to ornately turned Bilros beds and furniture. Casa da Padeira takes its name from the baker's wife of Aljubarrota who, so legend has it, single-handedly dispatched seven Spaniards. A frieze of *azulejos* on the bar in the sitting/dining room shows her thwacking one of the septet into the bread oven. Several centuries on, a more polite reception awaits you at this quiet B&B run by Senhora Pacheco. All is polished and pristine, and there are capacious yellow-striped armchairs and a sofa to settle into. The self-contained apartments (some with wheelchair access) are well furnished; bedrooms are a good size, sometimes there's an additional sofabed, and some of the bathrooms are brand new. No meals here, but a good restaurant in nearby Aljubarrota. Families will appreciate the games room with its pool table and the garden with its hotel-like swimming pool bordered by plants, sunloungers and seating aplenty.

rooms	8 + 6: 8 twins/doubles. 6 apartments for 2-6.
price	€50-€70. Singles €40-€55. Apartments €85-€120.
meals	Restaurant nearby.
closed	Rarely.
directions	Along EN8 from Alcobaça for Batalha. House signed on left on leaving Aljubarrota.

	Senhora Lina Pacheco
tel	+351 262 505240
mobile	+351 918 201972
fax	+351 262 505241
email	casadapadeira@mail.telepac.pt
web	www.casadapadeira.com

B&B & Self-catering

Map 3 Entry 66

A Colina Atlântica

Quinta das Maças, Travessa dos Melquites 3, Barrantes,, 2500-621 Caldas da Rainha

A friendly place which works its magic on many levels and is a good place to come if you seek tranquillity and simplicity. The house is surrounded by apple orchards and there's great walking in the hills. Dutch Ineke and Ton have travelled a good deal in India and Asia, have introduced a funky, laid-back décor here and offer a gentle and genuine welcome. Basic bedrooms, unheated in winter, are in the single-storey stables – plain tiled floors, pale walls, wooden ceilings, no frills. Back in the main house, the loft is a beautifully spacious relaxation room with wood-lined roof, cotton rugs and futons – and you can join a 'guided meditation' class before breakfast. Or unwind with some nurturing reiki, a gentle form of healing. Most nights there are delicious communal 'world cuisine' dinners in a dining room that opens, in summer, to a pleasantly unkempt garden with tinkling wind chimes and langorous cat. There's plenty to see, from hot springs to markets; if you're a group of six, Ton will accompany you to the monasteries of Alcobaça and Batalha, or to Óbidos and Nazaré. *Minimum stay three nights.*

rooms	4: 3 doubles, 1 single. Extra beds.
price	€40-€45. Singles €25-€30.
meals	Dinner with wine €12, by arrangement. Restaurants walking distance.
closed	November-April (open Christmas & New Year).
directions	Directions on booking.

Ineke van der Wiele

tel	+351 262 877312
mobile	+351 967 024958
email	info@a-colina-atlantica.com
web	www.a-colina-atlantica.com

B&B

Map 3 Entry 67

Casas de S. Thiago

Largo de S. Thiago, 2510-106 Óbidos, Estremadura

Don't miss hilltop Óbidos, a popular maze of cobbled streets softened by blue and ochre washes and romping stands of bougainvillea and jasmine. This is an old townhouse, completely rebuilt to retain the proportions and layout, without any crumbliness and filled with interesting furniture and knick-knacks. Views are over the town and up to the castle and, surprisingly, it is quiet, even though you are in a parallel cobbled street to the main 'drag' with its souvenir shops and crowds (but few cars). Traditional bedrooms, not huge, are filled with dark wood furniture, lots of chintz, gilded wooden ornaments, pretty beds and a homely, pleasant feel. You can choose to look after yourselves (there's a well-equipped kitchen and plenty of food shops nearby) or take the two-minute stroll up to the Castelo (Carlos Lopes's six-bedroom hotel) for breakfast. Carlos is twinkly and fun – especially when he has guests! There are some excellent restaurants in town and outside the walls; pop into the Castelo for a glass of the local cherry liqueur, *ginjinha* and a game of billiards before bed.

rooms	6 doubles.
price	€80-€85. Singles €70-€75.
meals	Restaurants nearby. Guest kitchen available.
closed	Never.
directions	Enter Óbidos through main gate. Reception at Casa de S.Thiago do Castelo so continue to end of street. House on right, below castle.

	Senhor Carlos Lopes
tel	+351 262 959587
fax	+351 262 959587

B&B

Map 3 Entry 68

Pousada de Óbidos/Castelo

Paço Real, Ap. 18, 2510-999 Óbidos, Estremadura

This pousada has one of the most spectacular positions in Portugal: it sits inside the 14th-century castle at the pinnacle of hilltop (touristy) Óbidos. A small cobbled garden with sculpted bushes leads to reception; brave the ramparts and you look down onto dappled ochre rooftops and winding streets. Swags of bougainvillea and ivy spill over dazzling white walls into secret gardens where cats stretch in the sun; enticing alleys lead through ancient stone archways. Beyond, the surrounding plain reaches to the sea. We think the incomparable views more than compensate for the mauve hues and stainless steel of the décor, and the slight touch of the institutional about the food and the staff. An excellent buffet breakfast is served in the light and airy dining room with its marvellous outlook fromy stone-pillared windows; dine in, or head off into town for the rest of your meals. If you're into medievalism, the split-level tower rooms will delight: steep stairs lead up from each small (windowless) hall and bathroom to a tiny stone bedroom with arrow slits for windows and a superb four-poster bed.

rooms	9: 4 doubles, 2 twins, 3 suites.
price	€190-€300. Special offers available - see web site.
meals	Dinner, 3 courses, from €30.
closed	Rarely.
directions	From the motorway follow signs to Óbidos & then Pousada.

Senhora Costa Sousa

tel	+351 262 955080
fax	+351 262 959148
email	recepcao.castelo@pousadas.pt
web	www.pousadas.pt

Hotel

Map 3 Entry 69

Quinta dos Raposeiros

Caminho dos Raposeiros, Marvão, 2640-065 Santo Isidoro, Estremadura

Surfing is Tiago's passion. Since childhood, he's searched for the perfect wave. Together with his wife, São, he spent two years looking for the ideal spot to live and here it is, perched on a hill. Views sweep down a pine-strewn valley to the beaches around Ericeira, one of Europe's finest surfing spots and a 20-minute walk. The views, the tantalising waves, the sun, the walks are very special. The modern apartments, neatly tucked in a low building of peachy coloured stone, cannot compete, nor do they try to. Fresh, simple, uncluttered, their style is clean and crisp, their colours bright and sunny. Think bold paintings, cool tiled floors, large French windows, sleek wooden furniture. The kitchen is small but fine for holiday meals, there are sofabeds for extra sleepers, and the terrace is large and perfect for sundowners. And, should you choose to be spoilt, São makes excellent breakfasts of fresh fruit salads, breads and pastries served in a sunny room. Spend days surfing, swimming, walking through orchards, tucking into seafood – then back to the pool to watch the sunset. Perfect.

rooms	4 apartments for 2-4.
price	€100.
meals	Self-catering. Breakfast €5. Meals by arrangement during summer.
closed	Rarely.
directions	From Lisbon A8 towards Torres Vedras. Take Mafra/Malveira exit towards Ericera. Leave Ericeira heading towards Ribamar; right towrds Marvão/Lagoa. House signed left; left fork then 2nd left. House 1km on left.

	São & Tiago Matos
mobile	+351 936 162638
fax	+351 261 856886
email	sao@quintaraposeiros.com
web	www.quintaraposeiros.com

B&B & Self-catering

Map 3 Entry 70

Casa do Paço de Ilhas
Santa Isidoro, 2640-068 Ericeira, Estremadura

Arty, funky, quirky – and a short walk from a beautiful surfing beach with courses. Margarida has lived here for years and her bohemian spirit fills the space. The walls in the bar are choc a bloc with posters, photos, prints, plates and paintings – some her own – and other eclectic but tasteful clutter; the mood is happy, young, unpretentious. Miguel, who is half-English, rustles up the freshest and most delicious meals with a Mediterranean/Portuguese slant: fish from the sea, herbs from the garden. Casa do Palheiro is perfect for families or surfing friends with its mezzanine bedroom; it has cobbled floors and a jolly kitchen with the *alambique* where firewater was once distilled. In Casa do Celeiro you may cook in the simple kitchen or on the little open fire; then eat out on the sweet terrace. Tiny Casa dos Azores has a multicoloured celing and is a delightful place for a couple. Outside, a shared barbecue area and space to cook and eat, a saltwater pool, shady spots in the garden and Zorro, the donkey. And there's a B&B room to which you may retreat for a flower-filled bath – bliss.

rooms	1 + 3: 1 double. 3 apartments: 1 for 4, 2 for 2.
price	€30–€70 (€150–€400 p.w.). Apartments €70–€120 (€400–€660 p.w) for 4.
meals	Breakfast by arrangement. Dinner, 3 courses, €30–€40.
closed	Rarely.
directions	On road between Ribamar & Santo Isodoro, north of Ericeira on road next to sea.

Senhora Margarida Ferreira Carrasco

tel/fax	+351 261 864962
mobile	+351 916 931222
email	ericeira@casadopacodilhas.com
web	www.casadopacodilhas.com

B&B & Self-catering

Map 3 Entry 71

Quinta de Sant'Ana
2665-113 Gradil, Estremadura

The quinta, now a wildlife reserve, was once owned by the crown and borders the old hunting ground of the kings of Portugal. You get three holiday homes here, all cosy, homely and liveable-in – especially Caseiro, the first-floor apartment in the main house; there's a country wardrobe in the main bedroom, and a lovely bedspread with ruffles. The old wine distillery sleeps four and backs onto the village street, so restaurants and shops are a step away, while Marreco, a purpose-built house for eight, stands at the top of the vineyard, beautifully private with its own lawn and pool. And there's a second pool, too, just behind the quinta, open to all. Attractive traditional-new architecture painted a Tuscan hue combines with a real working-farm atmosphere (it's all a-buzz at harvest time) to make this place special. Ann is German – her family created the winery 40 years ago – and is married to an Englishman; they give a big welcome to families and have six children of their own. And there's an exquisite chapel built in 1630. *Minimum stay one week in high season.*

rooms	House for 8. Apartment for 6. Cottage for 4.
price	€516–€2,042 per week.
meals	Self-catering. Restaurant in village.
closed	Rarely.
directions	From Lisbon, A8 north, dir. Torres Vedras; N8 exit 5 dir. Mafra. At r'bout, right for Tapada de Mafra. Through Vale de Guarda village; left towards Picão. Quinta on left.

	James and Ann Frost
tel	+351 261 961224
mobile	+351 967 604496
email	james@quintadesantana.com
web	www.quintadesantana.com

Self-catering

Map 3 Entry 72

Pensão Residencial Sintra

Quinta Visconde de Tojal, Travessa dos Avelares, Nº 12, 2710-506 Sintra (S.Pedro)

Many love the faded grandeur that envelops this family-run B&B. It was built on a thickly-wooded hillside as a viscount's summer retreat in the days when fashionable Sintra was a hill station to local and international gentry – and became a B&B in 1958. An original bannistered staircase winds up to the bedrooms. These are enormous with high ceilings, wooden floors and rather dated furniture and fittings; it all has a distinctly out-of-time feel; modern rooms are more functional. Ask for a mountain view. Downstairs is an enormous dining room/bar where snacks are available, but we'd prefer to sit out on the wide terrace (with tea and cakes in the afternoon) with its beguiling views up to the fairy-tale Moorish castle. And the garden is a delight: dripping with greenery, it has some old, old trees, a swimming pool lower down and a small play area for children. Multi-lingual Susana is a young, bright and caring hostess. The village centre with its numerous restaurants and shops is a short stroll away; for the more energetic, attractive paths lead steeply up to Sintra's castles and palaces.

rooms	15: 7 twin/doubles, 8 doubles. Extra beds available.
price	€50-€90. Singles €45-€85.
meals	Snacks available all day, from €3. Restaurant 300m.
closed	Rarely.
directions	From Lisbon, IC19 exit for Sintra & São Pedro. Follow signs to São Pedro & Centro Histórico. Hotel signed on right as you exit São Pedro, towards historic centre of Sintra.

	Senhora Susana Bezold Rosner Fragoso
tel	+351 219 230738
fax	+351 219 230738
email	pensao.residencial.sintra@clix.pt
web	www.residencialsintra.blogspot.com

Guest house

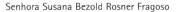

Map 3 Entry 73

Casa Miradouro

Rua Sotto Mayor 55, PO Box 1027, 2710-801 Sintra, Estremadura

The gaily striped walls make this an easy place to find as you wind down from
Sintra. The present owner left a successful career in Switzerland to launch himself
into restoring this light, elegant and airy home with views on all sides. Pass
through a palm-graced porch, and a handsome bannistered staircase leads you to
the bedrooms. Here antique beds and wardrobes stand on sisal matting; ceilings
are high and have the original stucco mouldings. It feels fresh and uncluttered,
helped by the size of the rooms, the two in the attic included. Views are to the sea
or to the hills. The sitting room has a similarly unfussy feel; here the sisal balances
the flounced curtains. There is a bar with several different ports, and a hearth for
sitting round in the colder months. Further downstairs is a modern breakfast
room, simply decorated with four round tables and giving onto a large terrace.
Classical music accompanies breakfast: cereals, cheeses, juices, yogurts, fresh
fruit, savoury and sweet breads. Frederic is a gentle-mannered, attentive and truly
charming host, his home as well-kept as any of Portugal's best.

rooms	6: 4 doubles, 2 twins.
price	€93–€130. Singles €83–€115.
meals	Restaurants 10-minute walk.
closed	Mid-January to end February.
directions	From Lisbon, IC19 to Sintra. Follow brown signs for Centro Histórico. At square by palace, right (in front of Hotel Central) & on to Tivoli Hotel. Down hill for 400m. House on left. Street parking outside.

	Frederic & Janda Kneubühl
tel	+351 219 107100
fax	+351 219 241836
email	mail@casa-miradouro.com
web	www.casa-miradouro.com

B&B

Map 3 Entry 74

Quinta das Sequóias
Estrada de Monserrate, 2711-801 Sintra, Estremadura

Hidden in its deep forest, this house is steeped in seclusion, rich flora and dream-like views of palaces and castles. This long, two-storey white Quinta, dating from 1870, is full of delights. Candida, warm and joyful, has a home of remarkable beauty inside and out. Corridors and walls are adorned with paintings and sculptures from some of Portugal's foremost artists, alongside fascinating older pieces from all over the world. Bedrooms are individual, with carved beds and polished mahogany furniture, rugs on tiled floors and carpets. The two bedrooms in the towers have beamed ceilings. The living room is long with comfy sofas, and overlooks the garden. Nearby is a library, and a comfortable stting room with games and lots of light. The breakfast room has a large open fireplace and tables large and small, and of course you may eat outside: Sintra is all slopes, and in front of the house the garden descends on lawned terraces, with pergolas and lush foliage, a burbling stream below and a swimming pool with views for miles. The people, the morning mists and sunsets are very special. *Minimum stay two nights.*

rooms	5: 2 doubles, 3 twins/doubles.
price	€145-€160.
meals	Salads & cheesboard from €15. Restaurants a short drive.
closed	November-February.
directions	From Sintra, follow signs past Tourist Office to Palácio de Seteais. Continue for 1km; Quinta signed on left, 2km up through forest.

	Senhora Candida Gonzalez
tel	+351 219 230342
fax	+351 219 106065
email	guesthouse@quintadasequoias.com
web	www.quintadasequoias.com

B&B

Map 3 Entry 75

Casal das Giestas

Rua do Alto da Bonita 112, Ranholas, 2710-185 Sintra, Estremadura

Plants with vibrant orange flowers clamber all over this pretty house and a jasmine-covered pergola overlooks the most fragrant of settings – a half-groomed, half-secret garden that the grandchildren call 'the jungle'. Your hostess is a mine of information about Portuguese society and history and enjoys having guests to stay. Her house, built in the 1890s, has many English touches: a kitchen dresser graced with English and Portuguese porcelain, an oval dining table, silver candelabra, traditional prints. Up a steep flight of stairs are bedrooms comfortable with antiques, good linen, rugs on wooden floors and plenty of Wodehouse novels. Classical music plays gently downstairs. A beautiful old plum tree offers shade among the layered terraces of wisteria, camellia, magnolias and old trees; at dusk, there's the hoot of the owl. Relax on the peaceful lawn in summer, three gentle labradors keeping you company. The village, vibrant with restaurants, boutiques and antiques, is a mile away, the Atlantic beaches not much further, and breakfasts promise homemade jams. *Minimum stay two nights. Babysitting available.*

rooms	3: 1 twin; 2 twins, each with separate bath.
price	€90.
meals	Restaurants 2km.
closed	Rarely.
directions	From Lisbon, IC19 to Sintra; to Ranholas; then uphill. Right after large house with blue & white tiles. House on left.

	Neilma Williams Egreja
tel	+351 219 234287
mobile	+351 939 596512
email	casal.giestas@oninet.pt
web	www.casaldasgiestas.pt.vu

B&B

Map 3 Entry 76

Quinta Verde Sintra

Estrada de Magoito, 84, Casal da Granja/Varzea de Sintra, 2710-252 Sintra, Estremadura

A modern house midway between Sintra and the beaches, set well back from the road, with distant green hills all around. This is a family home where Cesaltina, her husband Eugénio and sons Miguel and André create an easy, friendly atmosphere. Nature is bountiful; the house wrapped around by honeysuckle, palms, bay trees, cedar and succulents – breathe in the peace and quiet. Apartments have large sitting rooms, some with open fires and well-equipped kitchens and are set apart from the main house. Bedrooms have a mixture of wooden and metal beds, some antiques, pretty lights, matching fabrics on drapes and bedspreads, crisp white linen and tiled floors softened with small rugs. Bathrooms sparkle. Breakfast is taken at the rattan tables-for-two in the new conservatory breakfast room, or, on summer mornings, out on the terrace, next to the pool, with views of the lush Sintra hills. See if you can pick out the Moorish castle, Pena Palace, Monserrate house, the Quinta da Regaleira and Palácio de Seteais. It's a short drive to great beaches; fish restaurants too.

rooms	3 + 2: 3 doubles. 2 apts for 4.
price	€70-€100. Singles €60-€90. Apartments €100-€150.
meals	Light lunch available. Dinner €12.50-€15, by arrangement.
closed	Rarely.
directions	From Sintra for Ribeira de Sintra; to x-roads, pass tram lines to Café Miranda. After 1km, right for Magoito. After r'bout, left, then right. At V. de Sintra, after 1.5km, on right.

	Senhora Cesaltina de Sena
tel	+351 219 616069
fax	+351 219 608776
email	mail@quintaverdesintra.com
web	www.quintaverdesintra.com

B&B & Self-catering

Map 3 Entry 77

Quinta do Rio Touro

Caminho do Rio Touro, Azóia - Cabo da Roca, 2705-001 Sintra - Cabo da Roca, Estremadura

The Reino family have planted over 5,000 trees on their farm in the Sintra-Cascais Natural Park. Lush organic gardens heave with fruit — peaches, bananas, grapefruit, oranges, apples, plums, strawberries and, above all, limes. Feel free to pick your own. Scented jasmine tumbles over the entrance and other fragrant bushes tempt you into the gardens day and night. Your hosts are great travellers: having worked in the diplomatic field for many years their library reflects their travels, from Norway to Spain, Japan to Portugal; Senhor Reino likes nothing more than to help you plan your own journeys. The main house has an amazing collection of ancient pieces: Phoenician busts, Greek Amphora jugs, a classic Chapiter and art from all over. Choose between the rooms in the main house with their balconies, sea views and Portuguese tradition, or go for a more private room in the little house at the foot of the garden. The locally sourced and organic breakfasts are outstanding: home-laid eggs, local pastries, fresh cheeses, their own honey, ginza jam and pumpkin chutney. *Minimum stay two nights.*

rooms	5: 1 double, 2 suites, 2 suites for 2-4 with kitchenette.
price	€100-€200.
meals	Restaurants within walking distance. Occasional dinner.
closed	Rarely.
directions	From airport, A5 towards Cascais. Exit 12 for Malveira, Cabo da Roca, right. On for 8km; left for Azoia & Turismo Rural. 70m on, left again, signs to Quinta. 2nd house: stone wall with wooden door.

SPECIAL GREEN ENTRY
see page 16

B&B & Self-catering

Fernando & Maria Gabriela Reino

tel	+351 219 292862
fax	+351 219 292360
email	info@quinta-riotouro.com
web	www.quinta-riotouro.com

Map 3 Entry 78

Casa Buglione
Estr. Nova, 95 , Azóia, 2705-001 Sintra-Colares, Estremadura

You'll feel at home the moment you arrive, thanks to hosts Giampiero and Paul. They designed the semi-circular house themselves to make the most of the stunning sea views; the breakfast room is the best place from which to enjoy them. Breakfasts and dinners are delicious - your hosts ran a restaurant and know what they're about. Paul and his sister were also the figure skating champions of Switzerland: a picture on the mantlepiece shows their graceful dance on a frozen lake. The house is full of extravagent things from all over Europe, there are Louis XIII and XIV chairs in bedrooms, sumptuous bed linen, thick bathrobes, hand-painted doors, gorgeous antique mirrors and paintings from Italy, France and Switzerland. The village has some excellent restaurants and an atmospheric bar in a beautiful old windmill. Walk to the most westerly point of Europe, take off to the beach or stretch out on a lounger next to the lovely sheltered pool. Flamboyant and fun. *No smoking in bedrooms.*

rooms	3: 1 double, 2 twins (or 1 suite for 4). Whole house available.
price	€70-€90. Whole house €2,030 per week.
meals	Dinner, 3 courses with wine, €20. By arrangement. Restaurants nearby.
closed	Rarely.
directions	In Azóia head to centre. There, in front of Refugio da Roca restaurant, right up Estrada Nova. House 150m on right.

Senhor Giampiero Pedruzzi

mobile	+351 962 969471
fax	+351 219 282237
email	casabuglione@sapo.pt
web	www.casabuglione.com

B&B & Self-catering

Map 3 Entry 79

Convento de São Saturnino

Azóia, Cabo da Roca, 2705-001 Sintra, Estremadura

Deep in Azóia's valley something magical has happened. On the site of a ruin these talented owners designed a series of buildings based on a 12th-century convent. Whitewashed, inter-connecting spaces, curved roofs, winding steps, sparkling sea glimpses and a trickling spring – a place to lose yourself in. Bedrooms are decadently stylish, fabrics are rich, bathrooms are pampering. In the large lounge are squidgy sofas, coffee-table books, an old library and a collection of scrolls and artefacts found on the site. Help yourself to a drink from the honesty bar, then retreat to the high-ceilinged, candlelit dining room where the food is home-cooked and delicious (we loved the chilled melon soup with parma ham). Pad around the house, scramble down to the sea or recline on a rock and breathe it all in; the Convento feels restorative and spiritual. Add to this a shiatsu massage and your bliss should be complete. The atmosphere is more small hotel than private home but the staff are perfect and the beds with sea views are out of this world. Enchanting.

rooms	9: 3 doubles, 3 twins, 3 suites.
price	€120-€180. Singles from €120.
meals	Lunch snacks sometimes available. Dinner, 3 courses with wine, €25.
closed	Never.
directions	A5 Lisboa-Cascaís, exit Malveira & Aldeia do Junto. 4km after Malveira da Serra, left for Cabo da Roca. At Moinho D. Quixote bear right; signed.

John Nelson Perrie

tel	+351 219 283192
fax	+351 219 289685
email	contact@saosat.com
web	www.saosat.com

Hotel

Map 3 Entry 80

Casa do Celeiro

Pé da Serra, Colares, 2705-255 Serra de Sintra, Estremadura

It's wild and inspiring up here in the Serra de Sintra, a lushly wooded National Heritage site. The farm buildings sit serenely on their hill with views of azure Atlantic waters and sunburnt fields, and it's warm in almost every season. Mary and Alan, friendly, artistic and relaxed, are also the architects responsible for the renovation and extension of their 17th-century farmhouse. Upstairs is a two-storey conservatory, an easy place to unwind; below is Alan's acrylic jewellery workshop. Above the house is an elevated pool built on an *eira* (stone threshing circle) with panoramic views. But it's not just the setting that makes this place special, it's also the bohemian and laid-back feel: sculptures in the courtyard, paintings in every corner, books on art and design, easels, brushes, dozens of plants and quirky bits and pieces. Rooms are simple, with stupendous views. Breakfasts are communal and if you like to self-cater, there's a kitchen. The pool with views is open to all, so find your own space and relax. *Minimum stay two nights. WiFi available.*

rooms	4: 2 twins sharing bath; 1 twin with separate bath. Annexe: 1 double.
price	€70. Singles €45. Self-catering for 4-8, €800-€2,060 per week.
meals	Guest kitchen. Restaurants 2km.
closed	December.
directions	Lisbon-Cascaís; signs to Sintra via Azoia on coast road to Pé da Serra. Approaching Pé da S. fork, cream wall on right & small turning circle. Back towards Cascais & immed. left up steep road.

	Alan & Mary St George
tel	+351 219 280151
mobile	+351 962 447888
email	asgmsg@mail.telepac.pt
web	www.portugalpainting.com

B&B & Self-catering

Map 3 Entry 81

Casal Antigo

Rua do Cabo, 467, Malveira da Serra, 2755-159 Cascais, Estremadura

Eduarda's father said that one should 'drink' poetry, which explains why tea is served in cups printed with lines from the celebrated poetess, Florbela Espanca. For anyone wishing to pen a few lines themselves, this is the place for creative solitude. The area is as quiet as a convent – not surprising given there are two fine examples in nearby Peninha and Capuchos. (For restaurants and bustle, head to Cascais.) The original floors of the 200-year-old house remain, but there's no disguising the effort that has gone into this stylish suburban renovation. Four of the six rooms are suites, and all are graced with antique beds, but our first choice would be the one with a private balcony and an Atlantic view. Eduarda is friendly and efficient; she's an economist and used to manage Portuguese-speaking countries for the EU. A love of her native Africa is apparent in the objets d'art collected from her travels. Start the day with a plunge in the deep-blue pool, emerging for breakfast and no fewer than five different types of cheese.
Minimum stay two nights.

rooms	6: 2 doubles, 2 suites for 2, 2 family suites.
price	From €80.
meals	Restaurant 350m.
closed	Rarely.
directions	Passing Malveira da Serra towards Cabo da Roca, house 500m, on left overlooking the sea.

	Senhora Eduarda Cavaco
tel/fax	+351 214 852024
mobile	+351 919 472318
email	info@casalantigo.com
web	www.casalantigo.com

B&B

Map 3 Entry 82

Estalagem do Forte Muchaxo
Praia do Guincho, 2750-642 Cascais, Estremadura

Guincho is a long, curving sandy surf beach, backed by the Serra de Sintra – a perfect place from which to watch Atlantic sunsets. One of the best views is from Tony Muchaxo's inn, perched at one end of the beach. It's full of character, a fantastic combination of ocean liner and Neptune's grotto, with stone, cork pillars and strange wooden ceilings; floors are of *calçada*, parquet, slate, terracotta and marble, often sloping to adjust for the fact that it was all built on the ruin of an old fort. The restaurant has great ocean views and the building is arranged around an inner courtyard where sea birds land among the succulents; there's plenty of peeling paint, too, but then the ocean is fierce. Take a dip in the saltwater pool instead. In the bar find a wishing well with running water, rock 'booths' and tree-trunk tabletops and pillars. Bedrooms are large and comfortable; pay the extra for the sea views. You feel you're almost in the brine, and you hear the raging waves all night – an extraordinary mixture of wild nature, marble floors and beds with vinyl-padded bedheads. Eat in, or out in Cascais.

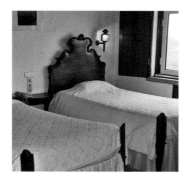

rooms	60 twins/doubles.
price	€65-€145. Singles from €55.
meals	Dinner from €25.
closed	Rarely.
directions	In Cascais, follow signs to Guincho. Along coast wide beach as road turns inland. Forte Muchaxo on curve on left, a little below road.

	Senhor António Muchaxo
tel	+351 214 870221
fax	+351 214 870444
email	info@muchaxo.com
web	www.maisturismo.pt/emuchaxo

Hotel

Map 3 Entry 83

Hotel Albatroz

Rua Fredereico Arouca, 100, 2750-353 Cascais, Estremadura

It's a big sprawling hotel and it's bang in the centre of Cascais, a full-blown tourist and yachtsman's village once known for its fishing. The driveway leads to tinted glass doors and Eighties-style reception hall and lounge. The main building of the Hotel Albatroz is the most conventional; more appealing are the Yellow House, perched high on the cliff and brand new, and the neighbouring home, the White House, attached via a floating walkway. What's special here is you have the feel of being in a small town – and, unusually, you get a choice of different bedroom styles. There's flowery English, charming Portuguese and Cape Cod modern – and the owners definitely take bathrooms seriously; they're stunning. We recommend the airy, serene rooms of the Yellow House with their wide-plank wooden floors, pretty fabrics and traditional tiles; the suite, with its claw-foot bath, steps down to lower lawn and pool, and exquisite ocean views, is spectacular. Dine on the terrace with views, stroll to restaurants and beach, take the train all along the river Tejo to Lisbon. Fantastic. *Wine tasting available.*

rooms	Main house: 40 doubles, 3 suites. Yellow House: 2 doubles, 5 suites. White House: 5 doubles, 1 suite.
price	€165–€565.
meals	Lunch/dinner €40.
closed	Never.
directions	From airport "2a Circular" towards A5/Cascais. Follow A5 until end, then signs for village centre. At train station square, up narrow street near BBVA bank; hotel at end, near beach.

	Frederico Simoes de Almeida
tel	+351 214 847380
fax	+351 214 844827
email	albatroz@albatrozhotels.com
web	www.albatrozhotels.com

Hotel

Map 3 Entry 84

Pousada de Queluz / Lisboa

D. Maria I, Lg. Palácio Nacional de Queluz, 2745–191 Queluz, Estremadura

You dine in the magnificently baroque Royal Summer Palace – 'Portuguese Versailles'. The pink pousada is on the other side of the courtyard, attached to the old *torre do relógio* – the clocktower – and has been beautifully renovated and revived. A dear little theatre, which would have been used for private performances, is now a space for occasional impromptu entertainment – truly charming with a gilded balcony and armchairs. Hotelly bedrooms have dark wooden furniture and raspberry and gold bedcovers, and bathrooms are big. Downstairs are a lounge, comfy with open fire, oil paintings, writing desk and bar, and a buffet-breakfast room, where tables are laid for two. Formal dining takes place in the Palace's grand old kitchen with its magnificent stone table and enormous central bread oven. Gold curtains hang at tall windows, there are bronze artefacts, sparkling, candle-dressed tables and a harp. A 20-minute taxi ride from the centre, the Pousada is not in the best area of Lisbon, but is worth the stay just for the Palace.

rooms	26: 24 twins/doubles, 2 suites.
price	€125–€195. Suites €179. Special offers available - see web site.
meals	Dinner, 3 courses, from €30.
closed	Rarely.
directions	From Lisbon, IC19 for Sintra; follow signs for Queluz & Pousada de Queluz.

	Senhor António Casa Nova
tel	+351 214 356158
fax	+351 214 356189
email	recepcao.dmaria@pousadas.pt
web	www.pousadas.pt

Hotel

Map 3 Entry 85

Rua Jeronimos 8

Bélem, 1400-211 Lisbon, Estremadura

Pasteis de nata, those crisp little cups of pastry filled with a creamy egg custard, can be bought from the Antiga Confeitaria de Bélem. And next door to that is World Heritage Site the Mosteiro dos Jeronimos, built to mark Vasco da Gama's discovery of a route to India. Olive trees, yellow trams, cobblestone streets, pretty waterfront and blissful Botanic Gardens – you are in the peaceful suburb of Bélem. Jeronimos 8 is the area's newest hotel, its 65 rooms spread over four limestone buildings from the 1940s, its façades beautified by Juliet balconies. Step inside to ultra-modernity and a cubist feel: curved white chaises longues and sofas, mezzanine levels and retro potted palms. Bedrooms display angular furniture and coffee and beige hues, French windows open to decked terraces, feather pillows are dressed in crisp cotton, bathrooms sport marble and chrome, TVs are flat-screen. There's a café for pastas and steaks, a terrace for the sun, room service round the clock. Not for those seeking tradition, but the staff are attentive and friendly, and there's comfort in spades.

rooms	65: 61 twins/doubles, 4 suites.
price	€160–€270. Half-board €40 extra p.p.
meals	Lunch & dinner €15–€40.
closed	Rarely
directions	A5 exit Bélem; down hill towards river. Left at sign to Bélem; then sign for Jeronimos; straight on, right at T-junc; 250m on left.

	Senhor Luis Cabrita
tel	+351 217 991930
fax	+351 217 930455
email	jeronimos8@almeidahotels.com
web	www.almeidahotels.com

Hotel

Map 3 Entry 86

Hotel Britânia

Rua Rodrigues Sampaio 17, 1150-278 Lisbon, Estremadura

Just one street back from Av. de Liberdade, this gem of a hotel was designed by Cassiano Branco and now ranks among Lisbon's classified buildings. Art Deco meets ocean liner: it is a museum piece. The fun begins in the reception area which sports twin ranks of marble columns, black and grey striped chairs, port-holed doors and a huge globe. During recent renovation, paint was stripped away here to reveal what appears to be a sea monster from Camoes' *Lusiades* (or there again, it may be Neptune); and there's more to be discovered. A wood and chrome staircase leads to the bedrooms (there's a lift too); these are enormous, with their own private entrance halls, original cork parquet floors, funky steel tubular lamps and original marble bathrooms with deep sinks and tubs. There's all the gadgetry that you'd expect of a four-star hotel and if the beds are period, the mattresses are new. The suites and rooms on the top floor are entirely new with wooden decking on private terraces. You can breakfast in your room if you prefer; it's a buffet that will keep you going all day, served by first-class staff.

rooms	33: 30 doubles, 3 suites.
price	€157-€350.
meals	Breakfast €14.
closed	Never.
directions	Follow signs to centre & Pr. Marquês de Pombal, then towards Praça dos Restauradores. Left just before Metro 'Avenida'. Rodrigues Sampaio is one street east of Av. de Liberdade.

The Alves Sousa & Fernandes Families

tel	+351 213 155016
fax	+351 213 155021
email	britania.hotel@heritage.pt
web	www.heritage.pt

Hotel

Map 3 Entry 87

Hotel Lisboa Plaza

Travessa do Salitre, 7, Av. de Liberdade, 1269-066 Lisbon, Estremadura

Right at the heart of things and yet shielded from traffic noise is this big, very comfortable hotel. The main attractions are all within reach and whenever you want you can slip back into sweet, air-conditioned peace – irrespective of whether it's baking hot or bucketing with rain. The hotel dates from the early 1950s and the expansive public rooms are well designed with elegant colours in fabrics and on walls, sweeps of glistening marble softened with rugs, even Portuguese tiles in the lift. Bedrooms vary in size and are a comfortable mix of old and new; bathrooms flaunt marble and big mirrors. It's everything you'd expect a capital hotel to be, the style coordinated and harmonious. Best of all are the staff, each one of them gracious, knowledgeable and friendly – an unexpected bonus. (And most speak excellent English.) The breakfast will suit most tastes, as will the buffet dining – though there are scores of other restaurants to try near the main Avenida. And the tour bus stops right outside the door.

rooms	106: 94 twins/doubles, 12 suites.
price	€156-€235. Suite €260-€450.
meals	Breakfast €14. Lunch & dinner €25.50.
closed	Never.
directions	Down Avenida de Liberdade in centre; at War Memorial, right into the Travessa Salitre. Hotel 20m from the Avenida.

The Fernandes Family

tel	+351 213 218218
fax	+351 213 471630
email	plaza.hotels@heritage.pt
web	www.heritage.pt

Hotel

Map 3 Entry 88

Heritage Av. Liberdade

Avenida da Liberdade, 28, 1250-145 Lisbon, Estremadura

Behind the elegant pale blue façade, this is a place of contrasts: light and dark, antique and boutique-chic. Built in 1779 on the site of a monastery destroyed in the earthquake, the building has been completely remodelled inside. Step down from the street to find yourself in a vast and lovely reception. Soaring walls are covered with *azulejos*, a poetic stairway winds up to a mezzanine library and tall windows give eye-level glimpses of Lisbon life. Take the lift and you'll feel as if you are outside again, for the floor is mock calçada and the photos are of local street scenes. As a counterpoint to the light and space below, corridors are subdued, velvety-brown and subtly lit. In stylish bedrooms, double glazing and shutters minimise street noise, colours are warm, leather-look bedheads reach to the ceiling, and there's every modern thing, from WiFi to flat-screen TV. Breakfasts – in your room or in the bar (but remember, this is Portugal: smokers are in evidence!) – are fabulous, staff are delightful, and the pool in the basement is the final treat.

rooms	42: 41 singles/twins/doubles, 1 suite.
price	€220-€320. Singles €206-€293. Suite €325-€550.
meals	Breakfast €14.
closed	Never.
directions	Hotel on corner of Avenida de Liberdade & Largo d'Anunciada.

	The Fernandes Family
tel	+351 213 404040
fax	+351 213 404044
email	avliberdade@heritage.pt
web	www.heritage.pt

Hotel

Map 3 Entry 89

Casa Joaquina

Rua Joaquina 5, 1150-197 Lisbon, Estremadura

A brilliant opportunity to live as a Lisboeta in a real Portuguese neighbourhood. You are free of tourists up here (except for those who meander up the wrong hill looking for the castle). Up a dozen cobbled alleys – or in the funicular, should the steps prove daunting – and you arrive at an extremely well-equipped little house for six, perched above the city's vibrant centre. Like the Tardis, the house becomes bigger inside, its several spaces linking into each other neatly. You get a spacious double room, a single with a trundle bed, and, in the basement, a cool, peaceful double (no window). Rooms have marble, granite and cork floors, smart black leather sofas and skylights for windows; everything is just so; even the plants are automatically irrigated. For views, there's a little roof terrace – not a bad spot for sitting out with a nice cold glass of vinho verde. Portugal's queen of fado, Amalia Rodrigues, was born just around the corner; now her nephew offers fado tours just for guests. And there's a great little greengrocer's down the street. *Minimum stay five nights. Ask about fado tours & culinary classes.*

rooms	House for 6 (2 doubles, 1 twin).
price	€245-€315.
meals	Self-catering. Restaurants within walking distance.
closed	Never.
directions	Above Praça dos Restauradores in Lisbon's old town. Detailed directions on booking.

	Debra Kleber
mobile	+351 913 464517
email	deb@visitingportugal.com
web	www.visitingportugal.com/casajoaquina.htm

Casas Pátria, Santana & Travessa
1150-197 Lisbon, Estremadura

Casa Joaquina's owners (entry 90) have three more apartments in charming Baixa Chiado. Just opposite Joaquina is a three-storey house for four: contemporary, open-plan, light from top to toe. There's a clever, funky use of space – and a cream sofa, an antique bed, a well-equipped kitchen (skylight-lit), and a lovely open-tread stair leading to a living room and fabulous roof terrace. No better way to start the day than up here, tucking into fresh pastries from the local café. Within walking distance, down another cobbled alley, are Santana and Travessa. From Santana's first-floor living room a grand view sweeps across tiled rooftops and shining river to the famous Rossio Square; from tiny ground-floor Travessa you can espy the majestic Igreja do Carmo, ruined in the earthquake of 1755. Expect a great little kitchen with chunky bar stools and an up-in-the-attic feel (Santana); a cool white bedroom and a carved Bilros bed (Travessa). Bed linen and towels are immaculate. Restaurants, bars, shops and history down the hill, and the beach a train ride away. *Min. three nights. Ask about fado tours & culinary classes.*

rooms	House for 4. Apartment for 2-4. Apartment for 2.
price	House €195-€240. Apartment for 2-4, €135-€160. Apartment for 2, €115-€135.
meals	Self-catering. Restaurants within walking distance.
closed	Never.
directions	Above Praça dos Restauradores in Lisbon's old town. Detailed directions on booking.

	Debra Kleber
mobile	+351 913 464517
email	deb@visitingportugal.com
web	www.visitingportugal.com/casapatria.htm

Solar do Castelo

Rua das Cozinhas, 2 (ao Castelo), 1100-181 Lisbon, Estremadura

The setting is spectacular – high up on the hill the hotel sits within the cobbled, car-free precinct of St Jorge's Castle overlooking Lisbon and its river. The building housed the kitchens of the first Royal Palace 800 years ago. It surrounds an inner courtyard and gardens and has ruins to explore. Décor is contemporary with a beautiful mix of materials: marble, tiles, textiles, parquet. Corridors have walls tiled in the Pombal star/flower pattern; expect a stylish honesty bar, wicker armchairs and chunky blue and grey pottery. Bedrooms vary in size but all are perfect with Matalaise bed linen and a welcoming carafe of port; those in the palacete are smaller but have more charm and better views, the two top ones with small showers. Some have exposed brick and timber walls, others stone; all display rich textured fabrics and linens, kilims and throws in natural blues, terracottas and browns. The courtyard garden is a pretty setting for breakfast at wooden tables surrounded by pots of flowers, the peacocks from the castle nibbling happily around you. A luxurious haven in the city.

rooms	14: 4 doubles, 10 singles.
price	€210-€310. Singles €196-€282.
meals	Breakfast €14. Restaurants 15-minute walk downhill.
closed	Never.
directions	Arriving by car, go to Largo Menino de Deus entrance, where security guard will tell you where to park. Hotel in car-free precinct above city.

	The Cardoso & Fernandes Families
tel	+351 218 806050
fax	+351 218 870907
email	solar.castelo@heritage.pt
web	www.heritage.pt

Hotel

Map 3 Entry 92

As Janelas Verdes

Rua das Janelas Verdes 47, 1200-690 Lisbon, Estremadura

In the old city, just yards from the Museum of Ancient Art, is this old, aristocratic townhouse; the great 18th-century novelist Eça de Queirós lived here. It is a perfect place to lay your head when in Lisbon, and from the moment you are greeted by the smiling Palmira and her staff you feel like an honoured guest. To one side of the reception is the lounge, with marble-topped tables (for breakfast in winter), a handsome fireplace, piano and comfortable chairs. Enjoy breakfast — or a candlelit aperitif — on the cobbled inner patio where a fountain gurgles and ficus and bougainvillea run riot. A grand old spiral staircase leads you to the rooms, some of which have impressive views of the river Tejo (book early if you want one). They are quaint with repro beds, flounced curtains and delicate pastel colours. Dressing gowns and towels are embroidered with the JV logo; instead of a 'do not disturb' sign there's a hand-embroidered little pillow that says 'shhh!'. A delectable small hotel, enlarged to include a cosy library on the top floor with honesty bar — and more fascinating views.

rooms	29 twins/doubles.
price	€190-€295. Singles €177-€270.
meals	Breakfast €14. Restaurants nearby.
closed	Never.
directions	A2 m'way over river Tejo, exit for Alcântara. Over r'bout; follow tram route for 500m. Hotel on right, close to Muséo de Arte Antigo.

	The Cardoso & Fernandes Families
tel	+351 213 968143
fax	+351 213 968144
email	janelas.verdes@heritage.pt
web	www.heritage.pt

Hotel

Map 3 Entry 93

Residencial Alegria
Praça da Alegria 12, 1250–004 Lisbon, Estremadura

This family-run guest house could hardly be in a better position, yards from the street life of the Avenida de Liberdade yet in a quiet palm-fringed square which belies its inner-city status. It's all been freshly-painted on the outside and you should approve of your room, too: "bright, cheerful, clean and basic" is how our inspector describes her favourite Lisbon digs. For the moment there is not much in the way of public space but Felix, the Alegria's likeable owner, has extended the ground floor into a larger breakfast room. The antique dresser groans with the weight of the crockery and the fresh coffee is good. Some rooms are a shade drab with tired-looking showers. Try to book our favourite room, number 114, which has been redecorated in a jolly mix of blues and yellows (see photo). The double-glazing is good news for light sleepers; the corridors have been painted in cheerful yellow and this and the shining parquet floors give the place a friendly feel. An inexpensive and central address, close to restaurants and the capital's attractions – the choice for those on a tight budget.

rooms	35: 20 doubles, 11 twins, 3 triples, 1 suite.
price	€38–€48.50. Suite €68.
meals	Restaurants nearby. Light snacks from €2.50.
closed	Rarely.
directions	Turn off Avenida de Liberdade into Praça de Alegria. House between police station & 'bombeiros', behind Hotel Sofitel. Nearest metro: Avenida. Underground car park nearby, from €18 per day.

	Senhor Felix Santos
tel	+351 213 220670
fax	+351 213 478070
email	mail@alegrianet.com
web	www.alegrianet.com

Guest house

Map 3 Entry 94

Hotel Métropole

Praça D. Pedro (Rossio) no. 30, 1100-200 Lisbon, Estremadura

You couldn't be more central – Hotel Métropole stands on Lisbon's lovely main square, in the Old Town, walking distance from central station and with great views of Castelo de São Jorge and the Alfama. Built in 1917, the hotel has been carefully restored so as not to lose its youthful charm. Black and white checked floor tiles, cream walls with a green stripe, swagged curtains and retro lamps in the lounge add a touch of glamour; there are comfortable chairs in pinks, greens and creams and the feel is relaxed and easy. At the far end of the lounge is the bar – a great spot for a post-prandial drink before hitting the town. Bedrooms at the front have suitably 20s furniture, French windows and balconies; you may breakfast here if you wish. Bathrooms have a new tiles in the old style and look sensational. A fun place to come and feel nostalgic about the old days. There's a huge choice of restaurants nearby and fantastic shopping. Staff are very friendly and happy to provide a map, a cup of tea or whatever you need.

rooms	36: 12 doubles, 20 twins, 4 triples.
price	€134-€180. Singles €123-€170.
meals	Restaurants nearby.
closed	Rarely.
directions	From airport, take shuttle bus 91 straight to hotel, or taxi (approx. €15).

	Senhora Clara Rodrigues
tel	+351 213 219030
fax	+351 213 469166
email	metropole@almeidahotels.com
web	www.almeidahotels.com

Hotel

Map 3 Entry 95

Mouraria

Castle Hill, 1200 Lisbon, Estremadura

A former family home on Lisbon's Castle Hill, this first-floor flat is spacious, well-equipped and good value. It is also homely and inviting – Ken and Carole brought up their children in this neighbourhood some years ago – and would be a great place for families or groups of friends. You have two living rooms with comfy sofas and throws, one of which has an open-plan kitchen and dining area, and French windows opening into a pretty walled garden with citrus trees and views. The three interconnecting bedrooms are fresh and spotless with a bathroom to share. Colours are restful and relaxing, there are two TVs, loads of DVDs, and a welcoming hamper with wine. A family friend who speaks English and lives downstairs will happily show you the street's shop and small bar. This is a hilly spot: up takes you to the castle (ten minutes), down takes you to the bustling Rossio (three). All sorts of information has been thoughtfully provided and there's so much to see; you're near the metro and it's a train ride to the palaces of Sintra. Leave the car behind! *Minimum stay three nights.*

rooms	Apartment for 3-5.
price	£390-£550 per week. Weekends from £250.
meals	Self-catering. Restaurants nearby.
closed	Never.
directions	Taxi from Lisbon airport (approx. €15) or go to Largo Martim Moniz. Walk up Escadinhas da Saude. Left at top, house 30m on left.

	Ken Parr & Carole Young
tel/fax	+351 245 964465
mobile	+351 916 324565
email	pomarv@gmail.com
web	www.pomarv.jazznet.pt

Self-catering

Map 3 Entry 96

Antiga Casa do Castelo

Rua do Espírito Santo, 2, 1100-224 Lisbon, Estremadura

Your own slice of Portuguese life – complete with outside washing rails so you can meet the locals. And it's right inside the Castelo de São Jorge: a short stroll and you have the best view in town. At sunset you might just find a fado singer. In the evenings the tourists head down the hill and you have the place to yourself – along with the local kids who love to play hide and seek in the nearby square. This place is perfect for an independent couple visiting Lisbon for a weekend. Your hosts thoughtfully leave a delicious welcome hamper for you, the kitchen's stocked with essentials and there's a tiny grocer's down the narrow streets where you can buy fresh bread morning and evening. It's absolutely gorgeous inside – tiny, but perfectly formed. An open-plan living room and kitchen, a leaf table for two, a small study and a bedroom in the eaves. Marsha and Tom have a flair for design – the flat is neutral, textured and beautifully decorated with soothing fabrics and soft lighting. Stay longer than just a few days and discover the faded grandeur of Lisbon – and its hills. *Minimum stay three nights.*

rooms	Apartment for 2.
price	€255 for 3 nights (€575 per week).
meals	Self-catering. Restaurants nearby.
closed	Rarely.
directions	From Lisbon airport, táxi to Castelo São Jorge, Rua Espírito Santo 2. From Lisbon in Praça Figueira, bus 37 bus to last stop: Castle; walk though castle arch up Rua Santa Cruz do Castelo to house.

	Tom Grigg & MarshaSmith
email	antigacasa@yourhomeinlisbon.com
web	www.yourhomeinlisbon.com

Self-catering

Map 3 Entry 97

Quinta de Santo Amaro
Aldeia da Piedade, 2925-375 Azeitão, Estremadura

Looking out to the Arrábida mountains, this gracious quinta was the family's summer house; now Maria lives here and opens her doors to guests. Bedrooms and apartment have a deliciously homely feel, and children will love the attic with its three rooms. In 'the middle house' are planked floors, panelled ceilings and attractive wooden beds. In the apartment, oil paintings and open hearths (a winter fire lit on arrival), period bathrooms and a piano. The lovely garden has shady walks and a discreet pool. It's the sort of place you won't want to leave. Breakfast is a help-yourself feast of homemade breads, jams, cheeses, eggs and bacon, Maria's oranges and the neighbour's strawberries — in season… But what makes it all so special is Maria herself, a lady with boundless enthusiasm and energy; she places a welcoming bottle of wine in your room and is full of ideas on where to eat and what to do. Lisbon is an easy drive, the beaches of the Setúbal peninsula are nearby, and the local Fonseca wine cellars are well worth a peek. *Minimum stay two nights.*

rooms	3 + 1: 2 doubles, 1 twin. Apartment for 6.
price	€90. Apartment €255 (€1,680 per week).
meals	Restaurants nearby.
closed	Rarely.
directions	From Lisbon, m'way for Setúbal. Exit for Azeitão, then Sesimbra; route 378 to r'bout at Santana; left to Azeitão on route 379 for 6km. At Café Estrela dos A., right for Estrada dos A. House at end.

	Senhora Maria da Pureza O'Neill de Mello
tel	+351 212 189230
mobile	+351 932 189230
fax	+351 212 189390

B&B & Self-catering

Map 3 Entry 98

Pousada de Setúbal

São Filipe, Castelo de S. Filipe, 2900-300 Setúbal, Estremadura

Climb up though ancient archways framed by old tiles – charming staff will carry your bags – to the 1590 fortress, built by King Filipe II of Spain. Setúbal Castle has the best views of the city below, but you can also see much further – ferry across the bay to the long white beaches of the Tróia peninsular. Climb giant stone steps to the top and ask to see the old chapel with its stunning *azulejos*. The pousada has been cleverly done up and feels intimate and friendly. Bedrooms have been beautifully decorated in greens and golds and are all individual – one has a sitting room on a mezzanine, the suite has a view-filled balcony and fresh fruit on a platter. There's antique carved furniture in the bedrooms and some lovely old wooden dressers in the hallway. The restaurant serves local seafish and regional food and has more fantastic vistas across the Sado estuary. Staff are very happy to advise on the best things to see and do, from boat trips to golf – and it's an easy train ride to Lisbon, so there's no need to hire a car. The Arrábida mountain range and natural park are also close by.

rooms	16: 8 doubles, 7 twins, 1 suite.
price	€150-€230. Special offers available - see web site.
meals	Dinner, 3 courses, from €30.
closed	Rarely.
directions	From the A2 follow signs for Sétubal. There, follow signs for Pousada.

	Senhor Miguel Castilho
tel	+351 265 550070
fax	+351 265 539240
email	recepcao.sfilipe@pousadas.pt
web	www.pousadas.pt

Hotel

Map 3 Entry 99

Há Mar Ao Luar

Casa do Mar e Moinho do Luar, Alto S. Filipe CCI3114, 2900-300 Setúbal, Estremadura

The vibrant Brazilian dancers in the paintings sum it up: this place is fun. And funky and charming. Stay in the windmill whose staircase, hugging the curved wall, winds romantically up from the circular living space to bed. Or take the beach cabana – French windows pull the sea views into the open-plan bedroom/dining room downstairs, there are twin beds in the attic (reached by ladder) for the children and colouful ribbons hanging from the doors. It's the kind of place where you won't mind getting sand everywhere. Happy summer holidays will be spent here and everything has been designed with the sea in mind – pictures of lighthouses, colourful tiling on the bathroom floors, hanging rails for tea towels, upside-down painted fish and buckets, whale-tail door handles, lobster pots and more. Breakfast waits in the fridge, fresh bread is attached to the door in the morning. White-sand views, peace, sea air – inspirational. Pretty gardens too and a lovely pool to cool off in. It's good value and you're very close to beautiful beaches, dolphins, boat trips – and, of course, the city.

rooms	1 + 5: 1 twin. Windmill for 2; house for 2; beach cabana for 2-4; 2 apartments for 2.
price	€50-€90. Windmill €100-€120. Cabana, house & apts €75-€90.
meals	Breakfast provided. Restaurants 1.5km.
closed	Rarely.
directions	From A2 for Sétubal centre; follow signs for Pousada de São Filipe. Up hill until sign for Há Mar auo Luar; 2nd on right.

	Senhora Maria Pereira Caldas
tel	+351 265 220901
fax	+351 265 534432
email	hamaraoluar@iol.pt
web	www.hamaraoluar.com

B&B & Self-catering

Map 3 Entry 100

Pousada de Alcácer do Sal

D. Afonso II, Castelo de Alcácer, 7580-123 Alcácer do Sal, Estremadura

One of the finest of the pousadas, a Moorish castle that dominates this rice-paddied valley. There was once a convent within its ruined walls; now the cloister has gone minimalist and the mood is more luxurious than ecclesiastical. This stupendous conversion combines generous spaces, multi levels and plentiful reminders of the building's origins with modern comfort. Patches of gilded carved wood, antique pieces, kilims and oriental carpets float on seas of cream marble, enhanced by white walls and modern art — a magnificent blend of modern and medieval, Moorish and baroque. It's cosy too, with huge red and blue suede sofas to sink into, and, in winter, a big fire in the bar. Sober bedrooms, all with views, have contemporary wooden furniture and textured fabrics for bedspreads and curtains. All 35 rooms fit beautifully into the old castle ramparts, yet there's still space for a pool and a little lawn, and a terracotta terrace on which you may dine. A last dash of style: many of the doorways are of warm speckled stone, remnants from the ancient castle walls.

rooms	35: 6 doubles, 27 twins, 2 suites.	
price	€170-€351. Special offers available - see web site.	
meals	Dinner, 3 courses, from €30.	
closed	Never.	
directions	From Lisbon A2, exit for Alcácer. Follow signs for Pousada.	

	Paulo Garcia
tel	+351 265 613070
fax	+351 265 613074
email	recepcao.dafonso@pousadas.pt
web	www.pousadas.pt

Hotel

Map 3 Entry 101

Ribatejo

Pousada de Ourém/Fàtima

Conde de Ourém, Largo João Manso-Castelos, 2490–481 Ourém, Ribatejo

The setting is the thing. In the heart of walled, medieval Ourém – a sleepy town of narrow streets and hidden gardens – this hilltop retreat has peerless views over rolling countryside; you'll feel like the King of the Castle. Hiding behind the small, bougainvillea-hung courtyard, the hotel is a conversion of three medieval buildings, including a hospital and servants' quarters. The mood inside is disarmingly light and modern. Sober but spacious bedrooms have clean-cut lines, pale colours, birch wood furniture, plenty of light; bathrooms are marble. Ask for a room with a veranda and a view. Fruit, chocolates and towelling robes add to the comfort. Reception rooms are cool and simple and include a small bar and a café-style dining room where good regional dishes are served. But outside is the place to be. There's a reading nook in a converted chapel and a pool dramatically sited just below the castle wall – a windy spot! Staff are friendly, making this a very nice place to recover after a hectic day discovering the delights of Fàtima.

rooms	30: 12 doubles, 18 twins.
price	€120–€180. Singles from €88. Special offers available - see web site.
meals	Dinner, 3 courses, €30.
closed	Never.
directions	From Lisbon IP1 north, exit for Fátima. From Fátima, a 30-minute drive, following signs for Ourém; there, follow blue signs.

	Senhora Conceicão Costa Sousa
tel	+351 249 540920
fax	+351 249 542955
email	recepcao.ourem@pousadas.pt
web	www.pousadas.pt

Hotel

Map 3 Entry 102

Quinta de Alcaídaria - Mór

2490-799 Ourém, Ribatejo

The wisteria-clad manor has been in the family for 300 years and is every inch the grand country house: stately cedar-lined drive, box-hedged gardens, 14th-century chapel. The main house is a cool, gracious building – light streams into lofty, elegant rooms with marble floors, arches and delicate plasterwork. Don't miss the chance to dine (inexpensively) around the enormous table; the chandeliers and china may inspire you to dress for dinner. An attractive self-catering house is just up the hill, while the B&B rooms are in the main building – and very special they are, too. Expect antique dressers, beds, comfortable chairs, perhaps a grand bathtub with clawed feet... there are beautiful moulded ceilings and big bathrooms generously tiled and marbled. Add to this great views, a peaceful pool and the natural kindness of your English-speaking host (Teresa may invite you to join her and her son for a glass of fine port) and you begin to get the measure of this charming place. Don't miss hilltop Ourém – a gem. *Minimum stay three nights in house & apartments.*

rooms	6 + 3: 6 twins/doubles. House for 4; 2 apartments for 4-6.
price	€90-€120. House & apartments €90-€137.
meals	Dinner, with port & wine, €25. By arrangement. Light snacks available.
closed	Rarely.
directions	From Ourém, towards Tomar. After 2km, road curves right; left at Turismo de Habitação sign.

The Vasconcelos Family

tel	+351 249 542231
fax	+351 249 545034
email	geral@quintaalcaidaria-mor.pt
web	www.quintaalcaidaria-mor.pt

B&B & Self-catering

Map 3 Entry 103

Casa da Avó Genoveva

Rua 25 de Abril 16, Curvaceiras, 2305-509 Tomar, Ribatejo

What strikes you on arrival is the serenity of the place. Huge old palm trees and pots of geraniums in the courtyard, a soft salmon and white façade – heaps of southern charm. José or Manuela usher you through to public rooms which are plush yet homely. In the living room is a large open hearth, comfy couches, a piano, a card table, family photos and books; in the dining room, dark antique dressers and a huge breakfast table – perfect *turísmo de habitação*. In the music room guests can take their pick from classical and fado to play; and the snooker room doubles as a library. There's also a small bar, well-stocked with Portuguese wines. And what bedrooms! Dark panelled ceilings, family antiques, good old paintings, stunning crochet; the doubles are up the old stone staircase, the lovely apartments are in a converted granary across the way. There's also tennis, and bikes to borrow, and a serene pool. You're off the beaten track yet minutes from historic Tomar, and near a reservoir with boats. Your hosts are kindly, educated people who delight in sharing this lovely, tranquil home.

rooms	3 + 2: 2 doubles, 1 twin. 2 apartments: 1 for 2, 1 for 4.
price	€75. Apartment for 2, €80; for 4, €140.
meals	Restaurant 3km.
closed	Rarely.
directions	From Lisbon A1, then A23, then IC3. In Asseiceira, follow 110 for Tomar; in Guerreira, left to Lamarosa-Curvaceiras.

José & Manuela Gomes da Costa

tel	+351 249 982219
fax	+351 249 981235
email	avogenoveva@sapo.pt
web	www.avogenoveva.com

B&B & Self-catering

Map 3 Entry 104

Quinta do Troviscal

Alverangel - Castelo de Bode, 2300-186 Tomar - Castelo do Bode, Ribatejo

If you love water, you'll love Troviscal. The modern villa looks over the vast reservoir at Castelo de Bode… such peace. Vera and João are an engaging couple with two teenagers and a pair of golden labs. Their house, on a secluded inlet at the end of a dusty winding track, is surrounded by pines, poplars and eucalyptus. The façade is traditional, the proportions are good, and the décor a smooth blend of new and traditional. There is a harmonious use of materials: American oak ceilings, slate floors, St Anna bathroom tiles. Beds are comfortable, rooms light and fresh, and glass-paned doors open onto a wonderful veranda where good breakfasts are served (homemade cake, fruit, yogurt, coffee or tea). The stone house has a cheery sitting room and a pretty terrace with furniture, pergola and barbecue. Laze by the pool, or stroll down the terraces and through the shaded pergolas – one a tunnel of wisteria, bliss in the spring – to the private floating pontoon; swim in the turquoise waters, bask on the sunlounger, slip off in the row boat. Special. *Minimum stay two nights at weekends.*

rooms	3 + 1: 1 double, 1 twin, 1 suite. House for 4-6.
price	€85. Suite €100. House €150. Extra beds €20.
meals	Restaurant 1km.
closed	Rarely.
directions	From Tomar or Lisbon, signs to Castelo de Bode. Straight on for 6km; signs for Quinta do Troviscal & Turismo Rural; after 2km, sign points to a track to right; follow to Quinta.

	Senhora Vera Sofia Sepulveda de Castel Branc
tel	+351 249 371318
mobile	+351 917 333456
email	vera@troviscal.com
web	www.troviscal.com

B&B & Self-catering

Map 3 Entry 105

Casa dos Vargos

Largo do Terreiro, Vila do Paço, 2350-202 Vargos, Ribatejo

Fiery red walls, gated entrance, vast courtyard, clock tower, private chapel – dos Vargos has it all. The 18th-century manor house with gothic additions has been Pilar's family home for 300 years. Grand but not grandiose, historic but not stuffy, the building is being restored – painted ceilings, pretty *azulejos* – to give the place a graciously comfortable feel. Traditionally furnished bedrooms, elegant with carved bedheads, soft colours and glowing floorboards, overlook the courtyard. Fresh flowers, rich curtains and antique mirrors make you feel grand and cosseted. Breakfasts of local cheeses and hams, fresh croissants and fresh fruits are served on the shady terrace at linen covered tables. Pilar has a fine eye for detail – and an inspiring wealth of suggestions for trips: Tomar with its Knights Templar connections, the hilltop castle at Torres Novas, the underground rivers of Candeeiros Natural Park. Return to a glass of wine in the shady peace of the courtyard. No swimming pool, televisions or tennis courts; the house and the owner are the attraction. *Minimum stay two nights.*

rooms	4 doubles.
price	€85-€100.
meals	Dinner €20. By arrangement.
closed	Rarely.
directions	Directions on booking.

	Senhora Pilar Tamagnini
tel	+351 249 791159
fax	+351 249 791139
email	info@casavargos.mail.pt
web	www.casadosvargos.com

B&B

Map 3 Entry 106

Casa do Patriarca

Rua Patriarca D. José 134, 2260-039 Atalaia, Ribatejo

The Casa has been in the family for five generations; the Archbishop of Lisbon was born here in 1686. You'll be greeted by Manuel's son, daughter or wife, and friendly dog. The sitting room has French windows opening to a walled garden; it's a long, low room, lined with sofas, comfortable not grand, a cool retreat. Just off here is a small kitchen for guests – excellent news for families not wanting to eat out. The long breakfast table is beautifully laid with home-grown fruit and delicacies, and juice fresh from their own oranges, and there's 'full English' if you prefer. Ground-floor bedrooms are homely and individually themed. Quinta has great-great-grandfather's bed; Oriente has lamps and cushions from India; Almirante is nautical in feel; Sana Sana evokes Mozambique – your hosts spent their honeymoon there. The much-loved gardens are a pleasure; an enormous date palm towers above the pomegranate, medlar, orange and fig trees, there are shady spots in which to sit and relax, and a pool edged by trees. Manuel and his family gently care for their guests and it's a treat to stay in this quaint little town.

rooms	6: 4 doubles, 2 twins.
price	€50-€75.
meals	Self-catering option. Restaurant 100m.
closed	Rarely.
directions	From m'way, exit 1 for Torres Novas, then IP6, then IC3 for Tomar. After 1,500m, signs to Atalaia & Casa.

	Manuel & Luisa d'Oliveira
tel	+351 249 710581
fax	+351 249 711191
email	mop59265@mail.telepac.pt
web	casadopatriarca.pt.vu

B&B

Map 3 Entry 107

Solar de Alvega
EN 118-km149, Alvega, 2205-104 Abrantes, Ribatejo

The Marquês de Pombal built it in the 18th century and it is as imposing as ever. Glamorous Maria Luiza and her English husband bought the house in 1998, have restored it to its former grandeur and introduced English and Portuguese antiques: Staffordshire figures and blue and white *faience*, grandfather clocks, Portuguese flags. Maria Luiza has restored many of the antiques herself, from letter-scales to Art Nouveau lamps. Grand bedrooms have polished parquet floors, tapestry rugs, tasseled silk curtains, antique washstands, beds with elaborate headboards… all put together with love. The tower room has a door to a roofed balcony, the best room keeps its original pink and black marble bathroom. In the walled garden, scented roses jostle with figs and courgettes, tomatoes spring up in surprising places, and views stretch to the stream, tall walnut trees and countryside. A precarious walk takes you to the waterfall that powered the old mill Maria Luiza hopes still to restore; her energy and enthusiasm for conserving this fine estate is undimmed. *Weddings held here; check before booking.*

rooms	5 twins/doubles.
price	€80-€90.
meals	Lunch €15. Dinner €20. By arrangement.
closed	Rarely.
directions	A1 Lisbon-Porto, exit Torres Novas; east on A23; exit Mouriscas. Signs for Castelo Branco & Portalegre. House 5km after exit from A23.

	Senhora MariaLuiza Mallett
mobile	+351 917 610579
fax	+351 241 822915
email	solaralvega@yahoo.co.uk
web	www.solardealvega.com

B&B

Map 4 Entry 108

Alentejo

Pousada do Crato

Flor da Rosa, Mosteiro Sta. Maria Flor da Rosa, 7430-999 Crato, Alentejo

You're in the middle of nowhere. This small, bright village on the northern edge of the Alentejan plain has been lived in since Carthaginian times and was given to the Knights Templar (their distinctive cross appears as a motif – even on the delicious restaurant puddings). The monastery and castle were built in 1356 and the pousada incorporates part of the old building, where bedrooms are beautiful, and the addition of a modern wing in warm pink granite. To enter, you must run the gauntlet of a dark, guano-spattered outside cloister (pigeons everywhere) but don't be daunted – inside, you'll be impressed by the imaginative blend of old and new. A tower has been converted into a sitting area and the bar is in a vaulted refectory with barley sugar-twist pillars, while the big new bedrooms are given a contemporary flavour by stylish use of wood, creamy fabrics and lots of glass. The restaurant, in an upper cloister, overlooks lawns and fruit trees; the food is fabulous. There's a cobbled shaded patio in the garden, too, and a big pool. This is a hot part of the Alentejo, so you'll need frequent dips.

rooms	25: 22 twins/doubles, 3 suites.
price	€170–€260. Special offers available – see web site.
meals	Dinner, 3 courses, from €30.
closed	Never.
directions	From Portalegre, N119 north towards Crato. There, pousada is signed in village of Flor de Rosa.

	Senhor Domingos Lameiras
tel	+351 245 997210
fax	+351 245 997212
email	recepcao.frosa@pousadas.pt
web	www.pousadas.pt

Hotel

Map 4 Entry 109

Tapada do Barreiro

Carreiras, Castelo de Vide, Castelo de Vide, Alentejo

The charming farmhouse sits 500m above the village of Carreiras, in the heart of the São Mamede Natural Park. The whole area is beautiful with wooded hills, rocky crests and fertile valleys running along the Spanish frontier. Gently modernized, this is a relaxed holiday home perfect for walkers and birders. The ground floor is given over almost entirely to a basic kitchen/dining room with a wonderfully rustic ceiling, where French windows open onto a terrace (great for sunsets!). The bathroom, with washing machine, is also on this floor. Upstairs are three good-sized, chestnut-floored bedrooms, two with great views, and a sitting room with log-burner. The tangled garden – with its tiny 'cisterna' plunge pool – leads into open hillside studded with olive groves and corks. Everything you could wish for is here: a shop, bar and restaurant in the village below, the hilltop village of Marvão for good eating out, the Apartadura lake for swimming and fishing and a fine golf course. Peter, who lives nearby, can take you on birdwatching and walking trips – and guests become friends. *Minimum stay one week in high season.*

rooms	Farmhouse for 6 (2 doubles, 1 twin).
price	€400-€500 for 2 per week. Extra adult €100; extra child (2-12) €50.
meals	Self-catering. Restaurant 800m.
closed	Rarely.
directions	8km from Portalegre & 6km from Castelo de Vide. Detailed directions on booking.

	Peter & Rosemary Eden
tel	+351 268 629899
mobile	+351 962 467875
email	peter_eden@hotmail.com
web	www.wildportugal.com

Self-catering

Map 4 Entry 110

Quinta da Saimeira

Vale de Rodão, bl2-cx3, 7330-151 Marvão, Alentejo

The setting is peaceful, there's a beautiful view of Marvão, and, on clear days, to the Spanish mountains. At noon Bonelli's eagles appear from their nest in the rocks above to soar in the warm air, and throughout the day, you can hear birdsong and the tinkling of goats' bells. Choosing the right epithets to describe this place is tricky: top-quality, minimalist, lavish, impeccable, stylish... Two delightful old houses, rebuilt and expanded, make up the accommodation. An enormous effort has been made to achieve high standards and style; in the kitchens everything is brand new, work surfaces are polished granite, hobs are ceramic. Bedrooms are simple and roomy, with wooden beams and very comfy, long, purpose-built beds, covered in big fluffy duvets. Michiel's big black and white photos adorn the walls. He's a professional photographer and will run workshops for two to four people. Through a busy planting programme, Magreet is creating soft garden spaces around the buildings. A highlight here is the sense of swimming to Spain in the infinity swimming pool. *Minimum stay three nights.*

rooms	3 houses: 1 for 2, 1 for 4, 1 for 4-6.
price	€59-€78.
meals	Self-catering. Restaurant 4km.
closed	Rarely.
directions	Follow m'way to Marvão. After Portagem, pass Jardim; 1st left; 1st right; 1st left. Follow small road to house (1.2km).

	Michiel Ibelings
tel	+351 245 993970
email	saimeira@saimeira.com
web	www.saimeira.com

Self-catering

Map 4 Entry 111

Pousada de Marvão/Santa Maria

R. 24 de Janeiro, 7, 7330-122 Marvão, Alentejo

Exit the narrow, cobbled street, enter the simple wooden door and hold your breath – the view will amaze you. The rocky landscape surrounding hilltop Marvão is savage in its beauty. This pousada, created out of two old village houses, takes full advantage of its lofty position; the restaurant, sitting room and bar have floor to ceiling windows; it's as though you're sitting on a cloud. Low beamed ceilings, simple decoration and friendly staff help create a cosy and relaxed family feel. Light, sunny, pretty bedrooms are modestly comfortable and are being revived: dark woods and chintzy curtains replaced with rattan furniture and apricot shades. Some have mountain views, others give glimpses into the winding alleyways of the medieval town. Room 312 is small but has a private terrace; suite 210 has the best views. Marvão is a gorgeous muddle of cobbled streets and dazzlingly white buildings, crowned by its castle – gaze into Spain from its rooftop. Then back for dinner, innovative and regional (goat with thyme cabbage, perhaps?) and those mesmerising views. Breakfast is superb.

rooms	31: 9 doubles, 19 twins, 3 suites.
price	€120-€243. Special offers available - see web site.
meals	Dinner, 3 courses, from €30.
closed	Never.
directions	From Lisbon follow A2 towards Spain. Exit Estremoz/Portalegre. Continue to IP2. Near Portalegre take N246. Right at Galucha, continue along N259, past Portagem. In Marvão follow signs.

	Senhor Domingos Lameiros
tel	+351 245 993201
fax	+351 245 993440
email	recepcao.stamaria@pousadas.pt
web	www.pousadas.pt

Hotel

Map 4 Entry 112

Pomar Velho

Galegos, 7330-072 Marvão, Alentejo

A rural paradise on the Spanish frontier… the tinkling of bells as the shepherd drives his flock home, the rumble of the mule cart further down the valley. A sense of timelessness pervades the 18th-century farmhouse in its five terraced acres of fruit, olive and cork oak trees — an ancient mulberry shading the slate terrace, perfect for an aperitif. From the pool, gaze at the spectacular São Mamede range; if the weather's not too warm, head off for the hills — the walking is great. There's a chestnut-beamed lounge with blue sofas and board games, and a spiral wrought-iron stair down to a dining room whose stone bread oven makes a fine open fireplace. And the granite grape press is as old as the house. Bedrooms are fresh with a French feel: blue limed furniture, big square pillows, crisp white beds. Bathrooms are spotless. Marvão Castle dominates this mountain village where many festivals take place; come in November for the Chestnut Festival when the council subsidises the wine! Carole and Ken have been here for years, have a rather fine wine cellar and love to cook. Breakfasts, too, are feasts.

rooms	4 twins/doubles.
price	€60–€80.
meals	Dinner with wine, €35.
closed	22 December–2 January.
directions	From main road to Spain, left at sign to Galegos. Through chicane in village, then, as road starts to descend, 1st track on right for 200m. Park at end of track & ring bell at gate.

Ken Parr & Carole Young

tel	+351 245 964465
fax	+351 245 964465
email	pomarv@gmail.com
web	www.pomarv.jazznet.pt

B&B

Map 4 Entry 113

Quinta do Barrieiro
Reveladas cx. 10, 7330-336 Marvão, Alentejo

Climb the stone staircase, pass the pond, fountain and cypress trees, to the marble-lined pool. At 700 metres, the views over the plains and wooded hillsides of São Mamede Natural Park are mesmerising and stretch to Spain. Here the outdoors is as enjoyable as indoors, particularly as it's dotted with Maria's arresting abstract sculptures. Architect husband José has rescued the five-hectare farm, turning limestone outbuildings into modern apartments without losing the rustic charm. On stony terrain, white and ochre limewash façades, pantiled roofs and beamed ceilings mix with dazzlingly light spaces, funky colours and fun fabrics. Compact but well-designed, bedrooms are curtained-off while the kitchenette is tucked behind cupboard doors. Imaginative touches – a 30s style armchair, a pretty lace curtain – add panache. Families will like the six-person Casa de Sequeiro, the house where the chestnuts were dried. Visit medieval Marvão, try watersports at Apartadura Dam, hire bicycles to explore the Park. Or swing in a hammock on your terrace with only birdsong to disturb the peace.

rooms	10 apartments for 2. House for 6.
price	Apartments €75-€125. Singles €60. House €180.
meals	Self-catering with breakfast provided. Restaurants nearby.
closed	Rarely.
directions	From Portalegre for Marvão, pass Povoção Monte Paleiros, follow mountain curves until a long straight. At x-roads, right at signs to Revelados & Quinta, before Povocação Alvarrões.

José Manuel Coelho & Maria Leal da Costa

tel	+351 245 964308
fax	+351 245 964262
email	quintadobarrieiro@netc.pt
web	www.quintadobarrieiro.com

Self-catering

Map 4 Entry 114

Quinta da Dourada

Serra de S. Mamede, Ribeira de Niza, 7300-409 Portalegre, Alentejo

Irrepressible Nuno has left careers in bullfighting and international publishing
to restore his heritage: a pretty farm in a very lush setting. He's charming too.
The main farmhouse and much of the land has been lost over the years but from
the remaining buildings your host has created an authentic and comfortable place
to stay. The low-pitched family 'chalet', the nucleus of Dourada, is linked to the
largest apartment by means of a terrace with a soaring roof, a semi open-air area
where you may linger over drinks — and star-gaze at an unpolluted sky. The
apartments are single-storey and rustic in style, with dark beams criss-crossing
ceilings and simple rugs softening black slate floors. Walls are white, spotlights
sparkle, sofas have throws and table lamps create a cosy glow. There are smart
white showers, teensy kitchenettes and white linen bread bags to hang outside
your door for the morning delivery. Pathways edged with dry-stone walls lead
to the remains of an old sweet-chestnut plantation and a blissful pool; suppers
from a superb restaurant nearby can be delivered to the door. *WiFi.*

rooms	2 + 4: 2 doubles.
	4 apartments for 4.
price	€80. Apartments €560 per week.
meals	Breakfast included.
	Restaurant 10-minute drive.
closed	Never.
directions	Head towards Serra de S. Mamede.
	Pass Solão Frio or Reqeungo. Signs
	on left after 2km; right for Quinta
	da Dourada.

	Senhora Nuno Malato Correia
mobile	+351 937 218654
email	quintadadourada@iol.pt
web	www.quintadadourada.com

B&B & Self-catering

Map 4 Entry 115

Quinta Azenha do Ramalho

Painel Ribeira de Arronches cx. 15, 7300-406 Portalegre, Alentejo

A house of surprises. Low and whitewashed, clinging by its toes to the hillside, it opens up to reveal vast sunny spaces with breathtaking views over the gentle slopes of the São Lourenço valley. In this former water mill, with stream tumbling below, the rooms make the most of the space while keeping a rustic solidity. The open-plan living area combines crisp modern furnishings with a cosy wood-burning stove and colourful *arraiolos* rugs; the kitchen would suit the most perfectionist cook. Beamed ceilings, whitewashed walls and kilims on tiled floors give bedrooms a comfortable simplicity, and delightful wrap-around decking means you'll be dining outdoors whenever possible. Set in the São Mamede National Park, this is fantastic walking country and the Anglo-Irish owners, great walkers themselves, provide maps, suggestions and information about the wildlife. Hilltop Marvão and Castelo de Vide are close; return to the lovely garden's olive and fruit groves and nod off in a hammock to birdsong and goat bells. Steep drops inside and out make this unsuitable for tots. *Minimum stays of three to seven nights.*

rooms	House for 8 (1 double, 3 twins).
price	€1,150-€1,550 for 8. €700-€900 for 2-4.
meals	Self-catering.
closed	Rarely.
directions	Vale Lourenço is 4km south of the peak of São Mamede. 14km east of Portalegre, 8km north of Alegrete. Detailed directions on booking.

	Catherine Hogan & Chris Jones
mobile	+351 966 740272/740173
email	info@azenhadoramalho.com
web	www.azenhadoramalho.com

Self-catering

Map 4 Entry 116

Casa de Assumar

Rua 5 de Outubro, no. 23, 7450-017 Assumar, Alentejo

Indalina returned from Lisbon to her parents' village to buy and restore the house she fell in love with as a child. She claims it was the *Gone with the Wind* pink marble staircase that won her heart. Situated in the cherry orchards of the beautiful São Julião Valley, Assumar draws city folk from Lisbon and Porto in search of tranquillity. An 18th-century stateliness belies the house's 1950s origins, although the garden geraniums and verbena appear subversively post-modern! Indalina and Mário love company. She is a superb cook and you may find a long lazy breakfast turning into a dinner of regional specials including dog-fish soup and a wicked almond pudding. Sophisticated bedrooms lie behind raw silk curtains, the beds luxuriously cushioned and finished by night with the plumpest of pillows. Choose 'Don Dinis' for size and street views of jacaranda trees. Honeysuckle candles add to the gorgeousness of marble bathrooms. It's a labour of love befitting the community too; forget your key and even with the house empty, a local senhora will be summoned with a spare. It's that kind of place.

rooms	6: 5 doubles, 1 suite for 4.
price	€80–€100.
meals	Lunch & dinner available. Restaurants 5km.
closed	Rarely.
directions	IP2 for Estremoz & Portalegre. Right at r'bout for Assumar/Arronches.

Idalina Abade & Mário Gonçalves Nunes

tel	+351 245 508033
mobile	+351 933 249863
fax	+351 245 508034
email	casa.assumar@clix.pt

B&B

Map 4 Entry 117

Pousada de Sousel

São Miguel, Serra de S. Miguel, 7470–999 Sousel, Alentejo

Gaze to the ends of the earth, and then a bit further. The views from the dazzlingly white hilltop pousada, just north of the marble towns, spill over the Alentejo plains, a carpet of olive groves receding to a blue horizon. Sunrise, moonrise, sunset… they take your breath away. Wisely, the hotel doesn't try to compete. Airy, bright and modern, it has wide marble corridors leading to rooms unfussily furnished – tiled floors, creamy walls and light, wooden beds. A simple rug, elegant chairs and floor length curtains add softness. You'll probably sleep with the curtains open – let the sunrise steal in over the balcony and wake you. Bathrooms are elegant and cool in pinky-white marble. Hunting is a passion here; hunting scenes and trophy heads decorate the walls while game features on the dinner menu. A wide terrace means every mealtime allows you to savour the views. The large, circular swimming pools – a separate one for children – are spectacularly set on the lowest terrace with plenty of room for loungers. Comfortable, laid-back, friendly – and thrilling at full moon.

rooms	32: 28 twins/doubles, 4 suites.
price	€120–€243. Special offers available - see web site.
meals	Dinner, 3 courses, from €30.
closed	Rarely.
directions	From Estremoz, N245 towards Alter do Chão. When you approach Sousel, Pousada signed. Outside town, on top of hill.

	Senhora Maria Amalia Vaz de Silva
tel	+351 268 550050
fax	+351 268 551155
email	recepcao.smiguel@pousadas.pt
web	www.pousadas.pt

Hotel

Map 4 Entry 118

Pousada de Arraiolos

Nossa Senhora da Assunção, Apartado 61, 7044-909 Arraiolos, Alentejo

What strikes you at once is the feeling of space – and the views, which are glorious. In this remarkable conversion of a 16th-century convent a new wing has been added yet nothing jars; all has been beautifully designed and meticulously integrated. Huge, restful *salas* are linked by long corridors floored in matt grey granite. No fuss, no clutter, and everywhere so peaceful! Bedrooms glowing with cherrywood have glass walls opening to private verandas that overlook lawns and an irresistible pool. Beyond: the hills, dotted with olive trees and grazing sheep. A magnificent patio has been built between the old part and the new wing, just beyond the dining room; a lovely light is reflected off the white walls of the terrace and the lovely, blue-tiled cloister. Staff, young, attentive and charming, make you feel like an honoured guest. Above the convent loom the castle walls: Arraiolos, a pretty, cobbled hilltop town, is the home of the ubiquitous carpets. Precious fragments of old ones, survivors from the days when they were still made from natural undyed wools, are on display. What a place!

rooms	32: 30 twins/doubles, 2 suites.
price	€150–€311. Special offers available - see web site.
meals	Dinner, 3 courses, from €30.
closed	Never.
directions	From Lisbon A2 towards Spain. Exit towards Arraiolos. Just outside Arraiolos, off road to Paria, down very steep hill, signed.

Senhor Paolo Garcia

tel	+351 266 419340
fax	+351 266 419280
email	recepcao.assuncao@pousadas.pt
web	www.pousadas.pt

Hotel

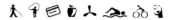

Map 4 Entry 119

Quinta da Espada
Apartado 68, Estrada de Arraiolos km4, 7002-501 Évora, Alentejo

Quinta da Espada: Quinta of the Sword. The sword in question was hidden on this farm by Geraldo Geraldes, who snatched Évora back from the Moors. With views down to that lovely city, surrounded by cork oaks and olive groves, is this peaceful, whitewashed, mimosa-graced farmhouse. Bedrooms vary in size and colour, and are simply furnished with delicately hand-painted Alentejan beds; terracotta tiles, *estera* matting and dark beams create a traditional country mood. Slate is an unusual and attractive alternative in the bathrooms, which are spotless. The Green Room occupies what was once the tiny family chapel, and the smaller sitting room, where you breakfast – or dine – before a lit hearth in winter, is particularly charming, its shelves crammed with Alentejan artefacts. You may be tempted by your friendly hostess's country cooking, but there is also a well-equipped kitchen for you to share with other guests. Leave the car behind and follow the tracks that lead to Évora from the estate – than back to the pool, bliss in summer.

rooms	7: 6 twins/doubles, 1 suite.
price	€78. Singles €48. Suite €92.
meals	Lunch & dinner €25, by arrangement.
closed	Christmas.
directions	From Évora towards Arraiolos. After 4km, Quinta signed to right.

Senhora Maria Isabel Sousa Cabral

tel	+351 266 734549
fax	+351 266 736464
email	isabelcabral@quintadaespada.com
web	www.quintadaespada.com

Pousada de Évora / Lóios

Lg. Conde Vila Flor, 7000-804 Évora, Alentejo

An intriguing juxtaposition – a 16th-century monastery rubbing shoulders with a temple of Diana. Inside the monastery, secularised into a private house at the time of the Dissolution, is another unlikely union – monastic architecture and baroque comfort. The bedrooms are small, their vaulted ceilings and religious pictures recalling a former life as cells, but there the austerity ends. They are authentically furnished with antique beds, brocade and lace aplenty, even flat-screen TVs. This gorgeousness pervades the rest of the place: 18th-century frescos (especially fine in the imperial *sala*) provide a backdrop for velvet plush sofas, brocade curtains, gilt mirrors, Arraiolos rugs, vases of intoxicating lilies... The arches on the ground floor are gothic, those on the floor above romanesque, with remnants of the Manueline scattered about. Part of the cloister, now glassed in, is a restaurant serving very good breakfasts and dinners, and staff are young and well-trained. Outside is a vine-covered cobbled terrace with a bar, rattan chairs and Moroccan lamps. Beautiful Évora waits outside the door.

rooms	36: 24 doubles, 7 twins, 5 suites,
price	€150-€345. Special offers available - see web site.
meals	Dinner, 3 courses, from €30.
closed	Never.
directions	From Lisbon, A2 towards Spain. Exit for N114 Évora. Follow signs to centre of Évora. Pousada is signed, next to temple of Diana.

	Senhor Paolo Garcia
tel	+351 266 730070
fax	+351 266 707248
email	recepcao.loios@pousadas.pt
web	www.pousadas.pt

Hotel

Map 4 Entry 121

Hotel Convento de São Paulo

Aldeia da Serra, 7170-120 Redondo, Alentejo

Superb in all respects, this massive monastery was built by Paulist monks who came to these mountain slopes in the 12th century. It is still imbued with an atmosphere of spirituality and calm, and the 54,000 hand-painted tiles that decorate chapel and corridors comprise the largest collection in Europe. A red carpet softens terracotta floors and sweeps you along to the rooms, each occupying two cells: luxurious yet uncluttered, in keeping with São Paulo's past. Bathrooms have brass taps and white marble; little cakes are put out for you when staff turn back the sheets before bed. The living rooms are no less interesting, filled with modern art and family heirlooms, atmospherically lit by oil lamps and candles, and there's a bar with billiards and cards. In spite of vaulted chapel ceilings, the dining room is an intimate setting for authentic regional dishes; staff are young and charming, breakfasts are lavish. Outside, a beautiful tiled patio depicting the four seasons, a shaded pool with a view, and walks through the wooded slopes of the 600-hectare estate. The setting is exquisite, the spirit soars.

rooms	32 twins/doubles.
price	€130–€195. Singles €115–€167.
meals	Lunch & dinner €60.
closed	Rarely.
directions	From Lisbon on m'way A6 for Madrid. Exit for Estremoz, then towards Elvas for approx. 5km, then for Redondo. Hotel 15km further.

	Senhora Maria Helena Passão
tel	+351 266 989160
fax	+351 266 989167
email	hotelconvspaulo@mail.telepac.pt
web	www.hotelconventospaulo.com

Hotel

Map 4 Entry 122

Monte dos Pensamentos
Estrada da Estacão do Ameixial, 7100-149 Estremoz, Alentejo

Christopher — half-English — came here often as a child. The white-walled house surrounded by vineyards was his family's holiday home, built in the 19th century but renovated in the 1940s by Raul Lino, creator of the Cristo Rei statue in Lisbon. In the 1960s Christopher's father, a famous author, made it a meeting place for writers and artists (he was a friend of Henry Moore and knew T S Eliot). Now Christopher and Rita have turned it into a *turismo rural*. Though warmly updated and comfortable it keeps its traditional feel, thanks to wooden ceilings, stone arches and tiled floors. Rugs and ceramics add colour and style, and bedrooms are quietly at the back. Outside is a free-form pool in a lawn dotted with shady trees, and two converted outhouses (one once a donkey shed): these are attractive apartments with small kitchenettes for light self-catering. For serious eating, Christopher has some good recommendations for well-priced Alentejan dining. He and Rita are easy, interesting hosts and have two bear-like but charming dogs. Great value. *Minimum stay two nights at weekends.*

rooms	3 + 2: 1 double, 2 suites. 2 apartments for 2.
price	€65-€75. Singles €55-€75. Apartments €85.
meals	Lunch & dinner with wine, €18.
closed	Never.
directions	A6 motorway, exit Estremoz onto N4. 50m Estremoz. At r'bout, head back the way you came towards Évora/Lisboa (under A6 m'way). At x-roads right, signed 'Turismo Rural'. House 50m on.

	Senhora Andresen Leitão
tel	+351 268 333166
fax	+351 268 332409
email	c.leitao@aiic.net

Map 4 Entry 123

Pousada de Estremoz

Rainha Santa Isabel, Lg. D. Dinis, 7100-509 Estremoz, Alentejo

A jewel of a palace, built for the sainted Queen Isabel of Aragon; you'll want to approach in a regal way. So don't go into town; follow signs to the *centro historico*, reach the castle walls and enter via the magnificent drawbridge. The pousada is in the former armoury and has a royal grandeur: high vaulted ceilings, elaborate arches, acres of red velvet and carpet, gilt, tassels and swags galore. The bedrooms, especially those on the first floor, are similarly sumptuous, stuffed with oil paintings and dark massive antiques. It's one of the most splendid of the pousadas, impeccably run by a glossy, attentive staff. The striking central courtyard is dominated by the castle keep; a small garden full of semi-tropical trees and shrubs leads to a swimming pool by the castle ramparts and views over the town to the plain. The restaurant is extremely good and you can get a proper cup of tea here – in a teapot! On the walls of the chapel are exquisite *azulejos* depicting the life of Queen Isabel and the nearby museum has a fine collection of folk art.

rooms	33: 30 twins/doubles, 2 singles, 1 suite.
price	€150-€311. Special offers available - see web site.
meals	Dinner, 3 courses, from €30.
closed	Never.
directions	From Lisbon, A2 towards Spain, exit Estremoz. In Estremoz centre, follow sign for Centro Histórico. Pousada signed inside the Castelo of Rainha Santa Isabel.

Senhor Domingos Lomeiras

tel	+351 268 332075
fax	+351 268 332079
email	recepcao.staisabel@pousadas.pt
web	www.pousadas.pt

Hotel

Map 4 Entry 124

Herdade do Monte Branco

Rio de Moinhos, 7150-390 Borba, Alentejo

Few places can be more tranquil than this estate, on the sunny flanks of a hillside near Borba. Well off the beaten track, the farmhouse and outbuildings have been converted into apartments by their architect owner. (Your Lisbon-based hosts may be around at weekends.) They are well furnished in Alentejan style with an arty feel: whitewashed walls, antique or repro beds, hand-painted tiles. Bedrooms are countrified, simple and spotless, with painted beams, stone floors and comfortable beds. Bathrooms are good, kitchens have microwaves only (except in the casa for eight), and breakfast is included in the price. Wake to birdsong and rustling trees. There's a pool, a large, rustic games room/bar and a dining room where you may eat by arrangement. The Herdade is near cork trees and forest and there's a lovely short walk to a freshwater lake hidden in the trees. On the edge of the Sierra you are spoiled for walks. Or visit the production centres of cork, wine and cheese, explore the prehistoric sites, go clay-pigeon shooting. A good spot for nature lovers and for families.

rooms	4 apartments for 2-8.	
price	€55-€90. Ask for weekly rates.	
meals	Self-catering with breakfast included. Dinner €18, by arrangment.	
closed	Rarely.	
directions	A2 from Lisbon, southbound, A6 eastbound; exit at Estremoz & join N4. Follow signs to Gloria & then to Rio de Moinhos. Monte Branco signed to right.	

	The Medeiros family
tel	+351 214 830834
mobile	+351 962 988099
email	montebranco@netcabo.pt
web	www.herdadedomontebranco.com

Self-catering

Map 4 Entry 125

Casa de Borba

Rua da Cruz 5, 7150-125 Borba, Alentejo

A gem of a house in the centre of lovely Borba, built by Senhora's family in the 18th century, surrounded by its estate (olives, livestock, vines). An extraordinary neo-classical staircase leads you to the first-floor quarters (ask for help with heavy bags: there is no lift) where fine bedrooms have high, delicately moulded ceilings and parquet floors softened by Arraiolos rugs. And there is no shortage of family antiques! The Bishop's Room (where the Archbishop of Évora stayed) has an 18th-century canopied bed, Grandmother's Room an unusual lift-up sink. There are claw-footed baths, elegant curtains framing windows that overlook a delectable garden, and jewel-like colours in furnishings and flowers. The sitting and breakfast rooms are similarly elegant; breakfast arrives via the dumb waiter. Your hostess is quietly charming and skimps on nothing to please you; at night, hot water to drink is delivered to your room, together with cake and a selection of teas. There's a long covered gallery, and a billiard room too. This is *turísmo de habitacão* at its best.

rooms	5: 4 twins, 1 four-poster.
price	€80. Singles €70. Extra bed €17.50. Cot free.
meals	Restaurants nearby.
closed	20-28 December.
directions	From Estremoz, N4 to Borba. House in town centre, close to post office (Correios).

Senhora Maria José Tavares
Lobo de Vasconcellos

tel	+351 268 894528
fax	+351 268 841448
email	casadeborba@hotmail.com
web	www.casadeborba.com

B&B

Map 4 Entry 126

Casa do Terreiro do Poço

Largo dos Combatentes da Grande Guerra, no.12, 7150-152 Borba, Alentejo

Once upon a time this long, dazzling white house was home to six families. There were just two old ladies left when João and Rita bought it, ten years ago; two rooms, 'Nana' and 'Rosario', are named in their honour. João is a lawyer but passionately interested in décor (he has an antique shop, too) and Rita is an interior designer. Perfectionists, they have remodelled the house and transformed it into a fascinating, even exotic B&B. Outbreaks of flamboyance – silk curtains, ornate bedheads, ragged walls, cut-glass mirrors – are saved from being 'over the top' by the occasional intervention of rough, natural stone, a simple colourwashed wall, and crisp unadorned linen... The house is in the centre of Borba, so views (apart from in the tower suite) are over the public garden at the front or the garden and pool at the back. Overlooking the pool is a long pavilion and a delightful area for guests to sit, while scattered trees provide plenty of shade. Breakfast is fresh and varied and the local restaurants are good; ask João about the wonderful adega nearby. *Minimum stay two nights in summer & at weekends.*

rooms	8: 1 double, 1 twin/double, 5 suites for 2, 1 suite for 4.
price	€75-€150.
meals	Lunch & dinner €20, by arrangement.
closed	Rarely.
directions	From A6 m'way, take EN4 and head into Borba. Follow this Rua de S. Bartholomeu and then after church, house on left (behind public garden).

Rita & João Cavaleiro Ferreira

tel	+351 268 808039
mobile	+351 917 256077
fax	+351 268 083624
email	geral@casadoterreirodopoco.com
web	www.casadoterreirodopoco.com

Guest house

Map 4 Entry 127

Pousada de Vila Viçosa

D. João IV, Convento das Chagas, 7160 Vila Viçosa, Alentejo

A monastic calm combines with gentle luxury in this restored former convent. Fragments of frescos, richly tiled dados and vaulted ceilings give a sense of history, in spite of modern enhancements, while piped Gregorian chanting adds to the mood. Built round a secluded cloister garden, some bedrooms overlook the cloisters while others overlook the town's patchwork of red roofs. All are a good size and have a fresh, understatedly modern style; white walls, rugs on polished floors, soft lights and brightly coloured fabrics. The suites are more elaborate, one with hand-painted bedheads, another with a cream-draped four-poster. Ask for a room with a pretty trellised balcony. The vaulted dining room is grander than the other main rooms and has a Last Supper fresco, baroque style chairs, gold colours and glowing terracotta. Good, traditional Alentejan fare is well served by bright young staff. In warm weather, eat outside in the atmospherically lit cloisters. With a herb garden and swimming pool, this is a blissfully peaceful place – despite being in the heart of 'museum town' Vila Viçosa.

rooms	32: 10 doubles, 20 twins, 2 suites.
price	€150-€230. Special offers available - see web site.
meals	Dinner, 3 courses, from €30.
closed	Rarely.
directions	In Vila Viçosa follow signs for Pousada.

	Senhor Anibal Coxexo
tel	+351 268 980742
fax	+351 268 980747
email	recepcao.djoao@pousadas.pt
web	www.pousadas.pt

Hotel

Map 4 Entry 128

Quinta Vale de Marmélos
7350-111 Elvas, Alentejo

Here you can see Spain from your bedroom window, across orange, lemon and olive groves. The wonderful gardens grow everything from figs to kumquats; the farm became a nursery almost by default when people kept asking for cuttings. It's a farmstay, set in a neo-gothic building with extraordinarily high ceilings. Friendly and impressively integrated in local life, Tim and Ann are English and formerly worked in Nigeria, this being their "last adventure". They strike a beautiful balance between being welcoming and leaving you to your own devices. Rooms have their own separate entrance and are simple and clean, furnished with Alentejan handpainted furniture; ask for the one with a veranda. Tim offers a guided introduction to the fascinating walled town of Elvas on the Spanish border (and lifts to and from town for evening meals and drinks – brilliant). Excellent value, this is ideal for gardeners, birdwatchers and anyone wanting to get away from it all. In the rambling, shady grounds are a pig, sheep, snoozing cats and, come twilight, a resident pair of tawny owls. Oh, and a brand new pool.

rooms	4 + 1: 2 doubles, 1 twin; 1 twin with separate shower. Apt for 2.
price	€55-€75. Apt £250 per week.
meals	Restaurants nearby. Dinner for late arrivals.
closed	Rarely.
directions	Lisbon/Badajoz m'way, exit for Elvas. Straight on until aquaduct; over 1st r'bout; right at 2nd r'bout for Olivenca. On past Santa Casa de Misenricorda; on left with flags.

Tim & Ann Claye

tel	+351 268 626193
mobile	+351 963 726237
email	annietimbo@yahoo.com
web	www.quintavaledemarmelos.co.uk

B&B

Map 4 Entry 129

Casa da Tapada d'Aldeia
Rua da Liberdade, 32, 7250-069 Terena, Alentejo

As Rita says, it turns its back to the lane. From the village side, you see traditional Alentejan houses, much as they have always been. Arrive through the tall gates, though, and you blink with surprise. Smooth white or rough golden stone walls, silver-grey terraces, flights of steps and pots of geraniums make up an enticing, harmonious enclosure. The immediate feeling here is one of quiet seclusion. On the fourth side, an unexpectedly big garden slopes away towards hills liberally dotted with cork oaks; a saltwater infinity pool, edged on one side with olive trees, is positioned to make the most of the view. Inside, the style is rustic chic and the bedrooms delectable with every possible comfort: fresh flowers, sprigs of lavender, rolled towels, soft pillows. Rita works as a lawyer in the parliament in Lisbon; if she's away you're well looked after by Catarina. Superb breakfasts are served on local pottery in the main house; in the guest sitting room, great windows are shaded by calico blinds. Rita is a sweet, gracious hostess and cares deeply about the culture of the area. *Minimum stay two nights.*

rooms	3 twins.
price	€80-€90.
meals	Restaurant 5-minute walk.
closed	Rarely.
directions	On N255 in Terena turn right to Hortinhas. In Hortinhas follow signs for 'Casa de Campo'. House at end of village.

Rita & Vasco Ataide

tel/fax	+351 268 459172
mobile	+351 967 357157
email	tapadadaaldeia@sapo.pt
web	www.wonderfulland.com/tapada

B&B

Map 4 Entry 130

Casa de Terena
Rua Direita, 45, 7250-065 Terena-Alandroal, Alentejo

In a sweet village, a seductive manor house. Stella and Jeremy lived in South Africa and their creativity has transformed the old place. Expect eclectic pieces and natural colours and textures in African wall hangings and unusual pottery – simple, stylish, chic. Bedrooms are fresh and comfortable in terracottas, olive greens, golds and creams, and blissfully cool for this sun-baked part of the Alentejo. This pair are natural hosts, love having people to stay and give you delicious food (if you pre-book). But go first for a sundowner and canapés at the Castelo de Terena and watch the 1,000-year old castle's walls turn orange with the setting sun. Uplighters in the downstairs sitting room have a similar effect on the wafer-bricked vaulting; wallow in sumptuous sofas before a monumental fire. Some bedrooms have views to countryside and lake, others have balconies and look onto cobbled village life. Spin off on a cycling safari picnic, try your hand at archery or visit the historical masterpieces of the area – Jeremy and Stella will show you it all. Deep peace in a remarkably untouched region.

rooms	6: 3 doubles, 2 twins, 1 family room.
price	€80-€90 Singles €65-€75. Extra bed €25.
meals	Dinner €25, by arrangement. Restaurants nearby.
closed	1 December-23 February.
directions	From Lisbon A6/IP7 for Évora, exit junc. 8 (Estremoz & Borba). From Borba, N255 to Alandroal & Terena. House in upper village, near to castle.

	Jeremy & Stella Doveton-Helps
tel	+351 268 459132
mobile	+351 914 739032
email	casadeterena@mail.telepac.pt
web	www.casadeterena.com

B&B

Map 4 Entry 131

Monte Saraz

Horta dos Révoredos, Barrada, 7200-172 Monsaraz, Alentejo

Monte Saraz is utterly beautiful. In an unsung region of Portugal, set among ancient olive trees below medieval Monsaraz, is a stylish cluster of whitewashed farm buildings — a stunning retreat. Dutch Marc, with a background in sustainable development, has put his rustic-minimalist stamp on 18th-century vaulted brick ceilings, flagstone floors and wooden doors, and made the place his own. Rooms glow with Indian kilim rugs, fine country furniture, beautiful examples of arts and crafts and washes of warm colour. All is cool and calm. There's a communal sitting room filled with flowers, three charming suites in Alentejan style with all-white bathrooms, and three delightful self-catering 'cottages', all with outdoor spaces. Outside are lovely orchards, gardens and peaceful shady corners; the pool, framed by the arches of the original olive press, is exquisite. Marc and son Ruben, easy-going, open-hearted and friendly, serve you delicious breakfasts Portuguese style, and the views of Monsaraz, perched on its hilltop, are stunning — particularly poignant when floodlit at night.

rooms	3 + 3: 3 suites. 3 cottages for 2-4.
price	€85. Cottage €525 per week.
meals	Restaurants nearby.
closed	Rarely.
directions	From évora, N258 to Reguengos de Monsaraz; then Monsaraz via Såo Pedro de Corval, 4 km before Monsaraz, left at sign to Olival da Pega and Monte Saraz, along track, through ancient olive grove. At T-junc., right; 1st group of houses.

	Marc P. Lammerink
tel	+351 266 557385
fax	+351 266 557485
email	info@montesaraz.com
web	www.montesaraz.com

B&B & Self-catering

Map 4 Entry 132

Hotel Rural Horta da Moura

Apartado 64, Monsaraz, 7200-999 Monsaraz, Alentejo

Monsaraz! It's one of the treasures of the Alentejo, an ancient hilltop fortress village of cobbled streets and whitewashed walls, visible for miles. On the slopes below lies this estate, its name recalling the Moorish invaders. The hotel's purpose-built extension to the old house has been beautifully done and has plenty of regional character: exposed stone and local slate, arched wafer-brick Moorish ceilings, rustic chunky beams. Suites and rooms are a good size, comfortable and attractive with traditional dark wood beds, monogrammed pillowcases and beautiful, locally woven rugs. The whole place feels reassuringly solid, and the thick walls keep you cool. Try the regional restaurant's meat and fish, the superb local wines and the good vegetarian dishes; take a drink to the circular bar with its rooftop terrace for fresh air with views. Further pleasures include a games room with billiards, tennis, a pool and, a mile or so down the road, the Alqueva Dam, Europe's largest man-made lake – sail off from the hotel's jetty. There's also an elegant horse-drawn carriage to ride, and horses and bikes.

rooms	25: 5 twins/doubles, 20 suites.
price	€85–€100. Suites €100–€125. Full-board €30 p.p. extra.
meals	Lunch & dinner €17.50.
closed	Rarely.
directions	To Monsaraz; just below fortress walls, do not turn right but follow road to Mourão. Signed.

	Senhora Sara Zambujinho
tel	+351 266 550100
fax	+351 266 550108
email	hortadamoura@hortadamoura.pt
web	www.hortadamoura.pt

Hotel

Map 4 Entry 133

Refúgio da Vila Hotel & Cooking School
Largo Dr Miguel Bombarda 8, 7220-369 Portel, Alentejo

Don't be fooled by the hotel's name: it is in the busy Alentejan town of Portel. Under the castle walls, in fact. The Vieira family have done a great job here and the once-abandoned building is now grand and infused with light. The designers have combined vaulted ceilings and character with a refreshingly modern feel, there's much exposed brickwork, and trompe l'oeil paintings on the first floor. The luxurious, spacious bedrooms have wooden floors, lush harmonious fabrics, generous beds and a cool, airy feel. Bathrooms are woody, and decked with fluffy white towels and robes. Five rooms have terraces with views of the castle; four 'garden' rooms are also terraced. Sitting rooms are comfortable and cool, and the very pretty restaurant is in the old coach house with stone pillars and a vaulted ceiling. Outside is equally appealing – plenty of shady places on the large lawn, several terraces smartly furnished, play equipment for children and a big pool. Sofia has always dreamed of owning a place such as this and now she has her own cookery school; the gardens supply the vegetables and herbs.

rooms	30: 12 twins/doubles. Annexe: 18 twins/doubles.
price	€80-€118.
meals	Lunch & dinner €25-€30.
closed	Christmas.
directions	From Lisbon A6 to Évora; IP2 towards Béja. Turn off for Portel & follow signs to Hotel Rural.

	Senhora Sofia Vieira
tel	+351 266 619010
fax	+351 266 619011
email	info@refugiodavila.com
web	www.refugiodavila.com

Hotel

Map 6 Entry 134

Pousada do Alvito

Castelo de Alvito, Apartado 9, 7920-999 Alvito, Alentejo

From the arched window of your bedroom, you look onto an unexpectedly green and park-like garden. Peacocks strut and call between the palms and there's an inviting swimming pool. The pousada is at the top of an attractive little town surrounded by olives, vines and cork trees. It's a 15th-century fortified palace, an intriguing mix of Moorish and Manueline architecture with a quiet cool interior. Only the restaurant is new and it fits in well – a low vaulted gallery with glassed-in arches overlooking the cobbled courtyard. The whole place has a pleasantly intimate atmosphere and staff are young and keen. Attractive bedrooms are enhanced by clever use of fabrics; the Queen's Room has a beautiful lacy stucco ceiling and a four-poster bed. Don't be put off by the unprepossessing approach, up a grimy flight of steps; everything else will please. From the tower and the battlements you can gaze on the town and the rolling countryside. This is an olive-oil producing area and in the summer it's hot, hot, hot. But, not far away, is the vast resevoir of Alqueva where you can fish, boat and swim.

rooms	20: 7 doubles, 12 twins, 1 suite.
price	€150-€311. Special deals available - see web site.
meals	Dinner, 3 courses, from €30.
closed	Never.
directions	From Évora IP2, then right onto N254. Through Aguiar. Pousada in centre of Alvito.

	Senhor Paulo J R Silva
tel	+351 284 480700
fax	+351 284 485383
email	recepcao.alvito@pousadas.pt
web	www.pousadas.pt

Hotel

Map 6 Entry 135

Herdade dos Alfanges

Apartado 5, Viana do Alentejo, Alvito, Alentejo

Follow a herd of 400 miniature Murcian goats through Iberian oaks and eucalyptus trees and you emerge in front of the startling white façade of a 17th-century working farm. Welcome to good living Portuguese style! Heleen is your gregarious, generous hostess, on hand to book a restaurant or to share a laugh. To ease you in gently, she offers guests a welcome dinner and a free shopping service. And there are endless diversions: swimming the black-mosaic pool, exploring the cathedrals of Évora, walking, riding, picking olives – even looking after the black pigs who are fed organic pig nuts and the best fruit and veg. Back in your house, sink into chunky furniture and warm your wintery toes by the old hearth and bread oven. There's a huge pine table for meals and a winding staircase to bed. Expect white feather duvets, soft lights, pastel-painted beams, fabulous towels – modern luxury and ancient character. In the barn studio are lofty ceilings and an ornate sunken bath – and the delightfulness extends to the formal walled garden with roses. *Welcome dinner on arrival.*

rooms	House for 4-7.
	Studio for 2-4 (let to same party only).
price	House €2,100. Studio €490.
	Prices per week.
meals	Self-catering.
	Breakfast by arrangement.
closed	Rarely.
directions	From railway crossing Vila Nova de Baronia, signs for Alvito; 2nd dirt road for 2km, bearing left as you see large barn & small house with grey sash windows.

	Senhora Heleen Rosa da Silva
mobile	+351 963 231407
fax	+351 213 940108
email	heleen@sapo.pt
web	www.alfanges.com

Self-catering

Map 6 Entry 136

Pousada de Beja

São Francisco, Lg. D. Nuno Álvares Pereira, 7801-901 Beja, Alentejo

Lazing in the big, quiet garden, surrounded by lawns, shady pergolas and palms, it's hard to believe you're in the middle of a city. The feeling of gentle calm continues inside; despite expert modernisation, this lovely former monastery still has a peaceful, unhurried air. The austerity of the massive white walls, vaulted ceilings and wide passageways is softened by serene colours and terracotta or dove-grey marble floors. Even in summer in Portugal's hottest city, sizzling in a vast, flat plain, you should be able to keep cool here – though the outdoor pool does get busy! There are several sitting areas – one in the chapter house – and the bedrooms are arranged on two floors around three sides of a cloister. Though not large (they were once monks' cells) they have comfortable beds, the finest linen, and marble bathrooms. The restaurant, in the old refectory, serves traditional, rather heavy Alentejan fare; breakfasts are excellent. Nearby is the convent where the famous *Cartas Portuguesas* are said to have been written by a nun smitten with love for a French knight she glimpsed from her window.

rooms	35: 34 twins/doubles, 1 suite.
price	€150–€230. Special offers available – see web site.
meals	Dinner, 3 courses, from €30.
closed	Never.
directions	From Lisbon, A2 towards Algarve. Exit towards IP8 Beja/Ferreira, pass Figueira dos Cavaleiros at the r'bout. 1st exit, continue along E802/IP2. In Beja, follow signs for Centro Histórico/PSP & Pousada.

	Senhor Paulo J.R. Silva
tel	+351 284 313580
fax	+351 284 329143
email	recepcao.sfrancisco@pousadas.pt
web	www.pousadas.pt

Hotel

Map 6 Entry 137

Pousada de Santiago de Cacém

Quinta da Ortiga, Estrada IP8, 7540–909 Santiago do Cacém, Alentejo

There's a good, old-fashioned Portuguese mood to your arrival at this quinta surrounded by mature trees and approached through cork forests and eucalyptus. Delightful staff live on site and, with only 20-odd rooms, the atmosphere is more home than hotel. A log fire blazes a welcome on cool days and the décor is suburban-stylish. In the main house, eight traditionally comfortable bedrooms have fitted carpets and wooden ceilings; the newer bedrooms are more 'Alentejan-rustic', though still with carpeted comfort. The apartments, in the chapel and garden, have two bedrooms each, a sitting room and a kitchenette for snacks. Four forested hectares are yours to explore and there's a handsome swimming pool in which to contemplate and cool off. A 15-minute drive brings you to some of the finest (and almost empty) beaches of the west coast; nearby Melides and Santo André have important saltwater lagoons popular with migrating birds. And do go to Santiago with its Roman ruins and cobbled streets leading down from the castle walls (but give industrialised Sines a wide berth).

rooms	21 + 2: 21 twins/doubles. 2 apartments for 4.
price	€120–€180. Special offers available – see web site.
meals	Dinner, 3 courses, from €30.
closed	Never.
directions	From Lisbon, exit A2 at junction 9 onto IP8. 10km before Sines, though woods, signed.

	Senhor Augusto Rosa
tel	+351 269 822871
fax	+351 269 822073
email	recepcao.ortiga@pousadas.pt
web	www.pousadas.pt

Hotel

Map 5 Entry 138

Verdemar

Casas Novas, Caixa Postal 1223, 7555-026 Cercal do Alentejo, Alentejo

Rustic holiday heaven in a bucolic setting, hidden among ancient cork oaks. Guest rooms are spread around the outbuildings but the hub of the place is the farmhouse and its dining room. The atmosphere is easy, and homely: a beamed ceiling, an open kitchen/bar, a comfy chair, and fun and good food shared at one big table. Dutch Christine and Nuno – a chef from Amsterdam – are utterly hands-on, swapping recipes with you as they prepare scrumptious dinner. Leading off the kitchen is the sitting room, equally cosy with guitar, paintings, books – a cool retreat from summer's heat. Bedrooms are simple, light, colorful and enlivened by Nuno's paintings; the cottages have chunky beams and open hearths. Heartening to find somewhere so ready to welcome families: not only is there a rustic playground, high tea and masses of space but ducks, cats, chickens, sheep and a donkey to ride – and beaches nearby. It's peaceful, friendly and refreshingly free of hotelly extras. The swimming pool is wisely fenced for safety, and the whole place is especially lovely in spring. *Casas Brancas member. Min. stay two nights in cottages.*

rooms	7 + 3: 2 doubles, 5 twins. 3 cottages.
price	€65–€85. Cottages €65–€130.
meals	Dinner €25, by arrangement (not Sundays).
closed	Rarely.
directions	From Lisbon A2, exit Beja Ferreira; N262 for Ourique. 500m after Mimosa, right for Cercal. 7km before Cercal. House signed.

Nuno Vilas-Boas & Christine Nijhoff

tel/fax	+351 269 904544
mobile	+351 914 583067
email	verdemar.cercal@mail.telepac.pt
web	www.verdemar.net

B&B & Self-catering

Map 5 Entry 139

Casa do Adro

Rua Diario de Noticias 10, 7645-257 Vila Nova de Milfontes, Alentejo

Come in June and the Festa do St António is on your doorstep: watch the folk-dancing from your street-side terrace. The Casa is in the middle of town – but quiet and peaceful – with a castle up the road and good fish restaurants round the corner. Friendly, kind, generous Doña Idalia fills the house with flowers – paper ones, silk ones and fresh blooms too. She has a fondness for big checks; most of the beds are covered boldly. It's a charmingly spruce little place, where paintwork is as fresh as a daisy and tiled floors gleam. Décor is traditionally feminine with modern touches; the dining room is Portuguese-pretty. Beds are antique or have painted headboards; one room has a terrace where pets are allowed. There's also a small kitchen for guests. Breakfasts are quite a spread, served all day on the terrace in summer; evening meals are typically Alentejan. Your hostess is a good cook, owns the café next door and serves you tea and delcioius cakes and pastries on arrival. Great beaches are near – both the sheltered sort and those with wild waves. *Free internet access. Casas Brancas member.*

rooms	6 twins/doubles.
price	€50–€75.
meals	Guest kitchen. Dinner on request.
closed	Rarely.
directions	From centre of Vila Nova de Milfontes, follow one-way system to beach, back up past castle to church, then left. House on right.

	Dona Idalia Maria Costa José
tel	+351 283 997102
fax	+351 283 997102
email	casadoadro@iol.pt
web	www.casadoadro.com

B&B

Map 5 Entry 140

Cortinhas

Vale Bejinha, 2581 Cx. S. Luis, 7630 Odemira/Milfontes, Alentejo

You arrive at the back... to what seems like a tiny house limewashed in ochre. Inside, what space! More than enough for four, and outside, a lush garden and a veranda with views. All is light and sunny inside, with soothing colours and unglazed terracotta floors. Your lofty, white-raftered living space is rustic and charming, with sofa and sofabed, woodburner, pictures and books; the kitchen is lovely. The powder-blue bedroom opens to a corner of the terrace, the twin room is white and cool. It is all very appealing, and homely. The owners live next door and Sophie's green fingers have nurtured the wisteria and plumbago that romps all over the house, herbs and flowers peeping in through every window. The garden leads to a meadow, a picture in spring, and a small lake two minutes away; all you hear are the tinkling of sheep bells and the occasional hoot of an owl. Behind, on the edge of hills, are a eucalyptus plantation, olives and oaks, good walks (which Tuke will guide or provide maps for) and plentiful birdlife. And the coast is 12km away. *Second house available in village.*

rooms	House for 4-6 (1 double, 1 twin, 1 sofabed). Extra bed available.
price	€60-€72 (€416-€550 per week).
meals	Self-catering. Restaurants 10-15km.
closed	Rarely.
directions	From Cercal, south for Odemira. After S. Luis, right at cemetery for Val Bejinha; 2km on, right at mail boxes, left at top.

Sophie & Tuke Taylor
tel   +351 283 976076
email   walkdontwalk80@hotmail.com

Monte Maravilhas

São Martinho das Amoreiras, 7630-427 Odemira, Alentejo

It is believed that the abundance of water here, in an otherwise thirsty region, is the reason why Monte 'Miracles' is so named. There are no fewer than four wells within the 22-acre estate and their water is sweet and drinkable. At the top of a long hillside track, the grounds are quite lovely, furnished with figs, vines and olive trees. Next door is a farmer who comes and picks the olives to turn them into oil, the grapes into wine and to dry the figs for winter. Such is the scene for these rather special houses (two of which inter-connect), the largest being the original farmhouse, all simply and stylishly converted by your serene host. The beams and the stone and wooden floors are as they were, while pale pine, huge stoves and white walls keep everything rustic and restful. Walking, cycling and painting parties are welcome, and Johanna is on hand to give a massage to ease any aching bones. Otherwise, relax in the shade by the saltwater pool. Meals are not provided but Johanna will cook by arrangement for groups; her only stipulation is that everyone washes up! *Minimum stay one week.*

rooms	3 houses: 1 for 6, 2 for 4.
price	€355-€590 per week.
meals	Self-catering. Restaurants 1km.
closed	Never.
directions	From Faro airport, A22/IC1 to Lisboa; exit Santana da Serra. Follow signs for São Martinho das Amoreiras. 1km before, take road on left signed 'Maravilhas'. Follow dirt track for 500m.

	Senhora Johanna Zijtveld
tel	+351 283 925397
email	info@montemaravilhas.com
web	www.montemaravilhas.com

Self-catering

Map 5 Entry 142

Monte da Moita Nova
Apt. 4424, 7630-055 Cavaleiro, Alentejo

If horse riding and unspoilt beaches are your pleasure, stay a week with Ute and Walter on their Alentejo farm. This exceptionally beautiful and unspoilt part of Portugal's Atlantic coastline has recently been designated a Natural Park; the eco-system of the dunes nurtures a huge variety of plant and animal life. You can reach the dunes, and hidden coves beyond, by walking 300 metres across Cavaleiro's pastures. The original homestead holds two apartments and the guest common room; the other two apartments, softened by a riot of climbers, have been newly built and horseshoe around a swathe of green. South-facing to catch the sun, each has its own terrace and they have a fresh and uncluttered feel: you benefit from architect Walter's clever use of space. Floors are of terracotta, sheets of good linen, beds of pine, there are woodburners and kitchens with the full self-catering kit. A wonderful spot to watch the sun dipping into the sea, and it's nice to come across a place which is so friendly to children. There are a paddling pool, beach toys and games, and you ride out on well-mannered thoroughbreds.

rooms	4 apartments for 4.
price	€65-€100 (€350-€570 per week).
meals	Self-catering. Restaurant 1km.
closed	Rarely.
directions	From Faro A22 to Besafrim. Then N120 to S. Teotónio via Aljezur, left here via Zambujeira to Cavaleiro. Here towards beach (not Cabo Sardão), & right after bridge to Moita Nova.

Ute Gerhardt
tel	+351 283 647357
mobile	+351 966 320640
email	moitanova@mail.telepac.pt
web	www.moitanova.com

Self-catering

Map 5 Entry 143

Monte do Papa Léguas
Alpenduradas, 7630-732 Zambujeira do Mar, Alentejo

Nearby Zambujeira do Mar is a small, fun place, popular with the Portuguese. Stay awhile in this privileged spot: a mile from bars, restaurants, shops and beach bustle. The rebuilt *monte* is a charming small hotel run by Teresa, ex-activity holiday guide, who provides mountain bikes, helmets, water-bottles and trail maps free of charge. She also organises riding – her own horses roam freely – and knows all about the cliff-top walks. Her bedrooms are typically Portuguese, with wooden floors, cane ceilings and calico covers on traditional iron bedsteads; fridges and TVs are neatly concealed behind doors, and there's central heating for winter stays. The contemporary studios in the newly converted stables are even more delightful. You share an honesty bar and a library of CDs, and, for those who have been up half the night acquainting themselves with the local bars, breakfast is served until 1pm. Under parasols in the palm-fringed courtyard, linger over a feast of hams, cheeses, eggs and homemade jams, cakes, breads and fresh fruits. There's even a saltwater pool. *Casas Brancas member.*

rooms	5 + 3: 5 twins. 3 studios for 2.
price	€65–€80.
meals	Restaurants 1.5km.
closed	Rarely.
directions	From Sâo Teotónio, follow signs to Zambujeira 2km before village, on right shortly after a road junction.

	Senhora Teresa Albarran
tel/fax	+351 283 961470
mobile	+351 919 618141
email	montedopapa@sapo.pt
web	www.montedopapaleguas.com

B&B & Self-catering

Map 5 Entry 144

Cerro da Fontinha

Turismo da Natureza Lda, Brejão, 7630-575 São Teótonio, Alentejo

Miguel has kept the character of these simple dwellings, while adding funky, chunky touches. And to reveal the different building methods he has left visible areas of *taipa* so you can see the mix of soil and stones between plaster and lath. Everything is as locally sourced and as natural as can be: showers with stone bases, bunk beds with carved ladders and fat wooden legs. Hooks for coats, towels and loo rolls have been created by embedding pebbles in the walls. Thick chunks of wood become mantelpieces, sofas have stone bases (cosily cushioned!). Work surfaces curve, there are alcoves for oil and vinegar, and cheerful stripes and gingham. Countryside on the doorstep, a eucalyptus wood for shade, organic fruit and veg delivered to your door and Carcalhal beach nearby; borrow a bike to get there. There are pottery and surfing lessons, a jetty onto the little lake (two loungers, two boats and a little water slide), a communal seating area, and outdoor seating for each house. Astonishing, inspiring — and fun. *Pets welcome in low season. Min. two to seven nights. Casas Brancas member.*

rooms	6 cottages: 2 for 2, 4 for 4.
price	€50-€90 for 2; €80-€110 for 4.
meals	Self-catering. Restaurant 800m.
closed	Rarely.
directions	From Faro A22 (IPI) to Lagos, then N120 for São Teotónio. 5km after crossing into Alentejo, left to Brejão, then 1st left. House on right just after lake.

	Senhor Miguel Godinho
tel	+351 282 949083
mobile	+351 917 802588
email	info@cerrodafontinha.com
web	www.cerrodafontinha.com

SPECIAL
GREEN ENTRY
see page 16

Self-catering

Map 5 Entry 145

Quinta do Barranco da Estrada
7665-880 Santa Clara a Velha, Alentejo

Hugging the shore of one of the Alentejo's largest freshwater lakes, the Quinta is heaven if you love wild beauty. The whole area has a micro-climate that keeps the water warm enough for a long swimming season and nurtures an amazing range of plant and animal life; visit in spring and the wild flowers will enchant you. Frank's eco-friendly renovation of the original low house took a decade and then a row of guest rooms was added. They are light, cool and pleasingly simple and their terraces have stunning lake views. The big extended lounge, dining room and bar share one sociable space and delightfully embrace Portuguese and English styles of décor; the food is organic. Beyond huge windows is a vine-festooned terrace for sultry summer days, while a further series of terraces have been planted with hibiscus, oleander, palm, jasmine, plumbago and cactus. Follow the path to the jetty where you can canoe, fish for crayfish, sail, water-ski or walk the shoreline, perhaps in the company of Frank's dog. Frank will help with the naming of all those birds; this little hotel is a birdwatcher's dream. *Casas Brancas member.*

rooms	11: 10 twins/doubles, 1 family room.
price	€70-€150. Singles €60-€135. Family €175-€300. Extra bed €25.
meals	Lunch €15. Dinner €25.
closed	Rarely.
directions	From S. Martinho das Amoreiras for Portimão. At T-junc., left to Monchique; 8km, left to Cortes Pereiras; 8.5km, right to Quinta. Printable map on web site.

	Frank McClintock
tel	+351 283 933065
fax	+351 283 933066
email	paradiseinportugal@mail.telepac.pt
web	www.paradise-in-portugal.com

Hotel

Map 5 Entry 146

Pousada de Santa Clara-a-Velha

Santa Clara, Barragem de Sta. Clara, 7665-879 Sta. Clara-a-Velha, Alentejo

In the Sierra, above the lake – what a setting! The vine-strewn terrace next to the bar has the dreamiest views... and red-rumped swallows, bee-eaters and butterflies. The building – not the prettiest in this book – was originally the house of the engineer who built the dam; for the last ten years it has been this pleasant retreat. Enter a sea of cool white marble and beyond, the warm restaurant; above are bedrooms with views. Those at the back look over the Monchique hills but the best look over the lake and have a tiny private terrace each. An apricot theme runs throughout, bedcovers and curtains match, the mood is harmonious and charming, the bathrooms are plush. Outside, pleasant gardens with hammocks and wooden swings lead down to a curved pool – and then to the turquoise lake for swimming, canoeing, water skiing. There are two restaurants in the village, but eat in at least once: the food is as delicious as it looks (seafood salad, grilled bass, honey pudding). Staff are pousada-professional, ready with info sheets on guided walks and bike rides, shooting and fishing.

rooms	19: 18 twins/doubles, 1 suite.
price	€120-€180. Special offers available - see web site.
meals	Dinner, 3 courses, from €30.
closed	Never.
directions	From Faro or Lisbon IC1; exit at São Marcos da Serra. Cross railway line; right for Benafátima. At T-junction right for Odemira; Pousada signed to right.

	Senhora Isabel Guerreiro
tel	+351 283 882250
fax	+351 283 882402
email	recepcao.staclara@pousadas.pt
web	www.pousadas.pt

Hotel

Map 5 Entry 147

Algarve

Casa Vicentina

Monte Novo, Odeceixe, 8670-312 Aljezur, Algarve

This west coast deserves visitors, not developers, and *turismo rural* is the answer. Sparkling new, rebuilt with sensitivity and imagination, the Casa is a restructed Taipa farmhouse. It has been extended and transformed, repainted with ecological paint, and has a very fine roof. Even the swimming pool is 'eco', the water lilies, rushes and papyrus guaranteeing a natural swim. Bamboo, plentiful trees and a sandpit slide have been planted by the thoughtful and charming owners; José is a retired civil servant and his English is good. Lovely big bedrooms have a Moroccan feel, with their lamps, cushions and colourful rugs; bathrooms are functional rather than stylish. Most rooms have French windows opening to the lawn or the olive trees and you can just glimpse the distant sea over the tops of the eucalyptus. The house is a wonderful summer retreat, its little outdoor sitting areas shielded by whitewashed buttresses, and there's masses to do – you can be at the beach within 20 minutes (take the bikes), and the walking is marvellous. *Casa Brancas member.*

rooms	8: 6 doubles, 2 suites for 2 + 2.
price	€60–€105. Suites €80–€135.
meals	Light meals available. Restaurant 2km.
closed	Never.
directions	From Lisbon A2 towards Algarve. Exit for Sines, Odemira & Lagos; follow signs for Lagos & Aljezur, exit just before Maria Vinagne; head towards Monte Novo.

José & Fatima Gomes de Almeida

tel	+351 282 947447
mobile	+351 917 762466
email	geral@casavicentina.pt
web	www.casavicentina.pt

SPECIAL
GREEN ENTRY
see page 16

Guest house

Map 5 Entry 148

Adega Velha & Casa Limâo

Salsa Verde, Joios, 8375-210 São Marcos da Serra, Algarve

Here is a peaceful winery in the undiscovered hills of the northern Algarve – close enough to raid the bustling southern coast and the endless surfing beaches of the west. It's just the place for a family, or two. Cherry and John lived here until moving to a house nearby and the rooms still bear the warmth and friendliness of their personalities: soft lighting, wood-burning stoves, deep armchairs, bamboo vaulted ceilings, a luxurious Dutch-fitted kitchen. Linked by a long and lovely veranda, Casa Limâo, a charming studio with a double bed, two single beds and its own kitchen, makes the whole place perfect for a big party; both houses have breakfast terraces with views, either over the pool or the small reservoir stocked with koi. Spread out below the old winery are its vineyards: John recently made his first vintage and it promises well. It's a deliciously quiet and private place and the magnificent pool leads to your own covered bar – perfect for a tipple or a swing in the hammock as you gaze down to the vineyard and across to the shimmering hills. *Minimum stay one week.*

rooms	1 studio for 4. 1 house for 4-6
price	£300-£1,200 per week.
meals	Self-catering. Dinner €25, by arrangement. Restaurants 5km.
closed	Never.
directions	5km north of Sao Marcos da Serra. Directions on booking.

	John Llewellyn
tel	+351 282 361286
email	cherry.lifework@gmail.com

Self-catering

Map 5 Entry 149

Inn Albergeria Bica-Boa

Estrada de Lisboa 266, 8550-227 Monchique, Algarve

A great place to unwind with massage, reiki, meditation… and delicious food, much of it vegetarian. All thanks to Susan, who has run this restaurant with rooms for years. Bica-Boa is the only inn in Monchique, its name inspired by the springs that well up on this wooded mountainside. As you wind your way up from the western Algarve, the exuberant vegetation will surprise you – and there are walks galore. Though the building stands just to the side of the road there is very little traffic, and the bedrooms are tucked away to the rear. Fresh, light and simple, with dark wooden floors and ceilings, they have super-comfortable mattresses and views across the valley. There is a quiet little guest sitting room with the same view and a homely feel: corner chimney, *azulejo*-clad walls and a table set for chess. The restaurant is popular with locals and ex-pats up from the coast. You get terraces for outdoor dining when the weather is right, a terraced garden with shady corners and a tiny pool. Staff are delightful. *Alternative health courses available.*

rooms	4 twins.
price	€53–€63.
meals	Lunch & dinner €15–€20.
closed	Rarely.
directions	From Faro, N125 west for Lagos. Exit for Monchique. Follow signs for Lisboa through town. Inn 300m after town on right, signed.

	Susan Clare Cassidy
tel	+351 282 912271
fax	+351 282 912360
email	bica-boa@sapo.pt

Restaurant with rooms

Map 5 Entry 150

Cabana dos Rouxinois

Apt. 33, 8550 Monchique, Algarve

Great swathes of the Algarve coast have been consumed by developers and concrete-pourers; up in these hills, a half hour from the coast, it doesn't seem to matter. The house and pool have some of the best views in the Algarve – its splendid gardens are a haven of peace. The house is on several levels: enter at the back, step down to the living room and thence to the terrace. You will be immediately captivated by the light, the space and the comfort. Everywhere are soft colours, good furniture, watercolours and colourful ceramics. Bedrooms, too, are lovely; one has blue toile de Jouy fabric, blue and white painted furniture and a matching bathroom that opens onto the main terrace, another a pretty pink and white theme, its own entrance and Alentejan painted furniture and bed. There's also a three-bedroom cottage. Maria and António look after you very well – you buy the food, they do the cooking. They also do the laundry, the cleaning and check the pool every day; they can babysit too. It's lavish yet elegant – the house belongs to an 'old' English family and little expense has been spared.

rooms	House for 8-10. Cottage for 5.
price	£1,000–£3,000 per week.
meals	Self-catering. Housekeeper cooks on request. Restaurants nearby.
closed	Rarely.
directions	From Faro A22 for Portimão & Lagos to Monchique. From centre of Monchique towards Foia. Left opposite 'A Rampa' restaurant & on down to house.

	Pippa Dennis
tel	+351 282 912822
fax	+351 282 912822
email	ferran@monchique.com
web	www.cabanadosrouxinois.com

Self-catering

Map 5 Entry 151

Monte Velho Nature Resort
Bordeira, 8670-230 Carrapateira, Algarve

Near to one of best surfing beaches in Portugal is this stylish, ecological nature resort – the rolling breakers can be seen from the house. Henrique, his partner and their young family are warm and friendly and know all the surfing spots. Splashes of orange, blue, violet, ochre and red – not forgetting some lovely hand-painted fish – fill this simple place with fun and good humour. Polished floors, Indian beds, floaty fabrics, bold art, sofas with plump cushions, warm lighting, music, books and magazines add to the sense of ease. A Morroccan mood hangs in the air. Suites face south and have their own private terraces with hammocks, lanterns and rattan chairs, and each is different; some have mezzanines, others woodburning stoves, all have sitting rooms. Big windows pull in the views and the peace is total – you are in a wild, empty, bird-rich natural park. Come evening, the west coast sunsets are inspiring, the stars dazzling. Get to the beach by donkey, take a surfing lesson or a boat trip, return for massage, yoga or tai chi. A sybarite's paradise. *Minimum stay seven nights July / August.*

rooms	9: 2 doubles, 7 suites for 2-3.
price	€100–€120.
meals	Kitchen on request. Restaurants nearby.
closed	Rarely.
directions	From Lagos, N125 to Vila do Bispo; N268 for Aljezur & Sines. Right at sign to Vilarinha; after 800m, left to Monte Velho.

Senhor Henrique Balsemão
tel/fax	+351 282 973207
mobile	+351 966 007950
email	montevelho.carrapateira@gmail.com
web	www.wonderfulland.com/montevelho

Hotel

Map 5 Entry 152

Pousada de Sagres
Infante, 8650–385 Sagres, Algarve

In the fifth century BC Sagres was "a meeting place for the gods, and forbidden to mankind". Well, mankind came and Sagres has a great history; Henry the Navigator established the Escola Nautica here, and Portugal began its rule of the world. The pousada, whose 1960s origins set alarm bells ringing, is remarkably sympathetic to its environment, and lies low on the cliff top, above a sea that clashes audibly on a wild day; the storms and the sunsets are thrilling. It has had a facelift under the new Pestana Group influence: pleasant colours, crisp linen, wooden floors. Ask for one of the older rooms with views over the pool and to the sea. The public rooms are beautifully done – choice antiques and comfortable armchairs, a sensational tapestry – and there's a games room for children, with bean bags; great to sink into but impossible to get out of. In the restaurant the fish, meat and vegetables are locally sourced. Everyone loves Sagres, with its attractive working harbour full of fishing boats and not a yacht in sight. Fish, surf, windsurf, watch migrating birds – or just loaf about.

rooms	51: 50 doubles, 1 suite.
price	€120-€230. Special offers available - see web site.
meals	Dinner, 3 courses, from €25.
closed	Never.
directions	From Faro IC4 for Lagos. There, N125 to Vila do Bispo. There, N268 towards Sagres; follow signs for Pousada.

	Senhor João Portugal
tel	+351 282 620240
fax	+351 282 624225
email	recepcao.infante@pousadas.pt
web	www.pousadas.pt

Hotel

Map 5 Entry 153

Romantik Villa Vivenda Felicidade
8650-191 Salema, Algarve

In the village you can still watch the fishermen mending their nets at the end of the day. The house on the hill, one of several built 20 years ago, now surrounded by a manicured garden of palms and pretty corners, has a view of the ocean from every room. Lie in a hammock, relax in the shade, take a dip in the pool; it's as peaceful as can be and the temperatures are mild here even in winter. Pristine modern bedrooms, each with white or cream walls or faux brickwork tiles, space (just) for chairs and a table, and glass windows that slide open to a veranda, are kitted out with fridges (breakfast basics provided), heated towel rails and satellite TV, while the spacious suite has a formica kitchenette. Brazilian Lisa and her German husband live on site and keep everything in order. Salema has several restaurants and bars and, best of all, a sandy, gently-sloping beach. Hop on the bus and head for the historic town of Lagos and its marina, or Sagres, perched at the extreme western point of Europe – the sunsets are marvellous. Golf courses are a ten-minute drive. *Minimum stay two nights.*

rooms	4: 3 doubles; 1 suite for 2 (with kitchnette).
price	€70-€80. Suite €90-€110 (€770 per week, May-Nov only).
meals	Restaurants in village.
closed	December-February.
directions	On the very top of the Urbanisation Beach Villas in Salema.

	Lisa Steiner
tel	+351 282 695670
mobile	+351 967 059806
email	romantikvilla@sapo.pt
web	www.romantikvilla.com

B&B & Self-catering

Map 5 Entry 154

Monte Rosa

Lagoa da Rosa, 8600-016 Barão de S. João, Algarve

In four hectares of unspoilt Algarve hinterland, Dutch Sandra has converted the old farmstead into a well-organised but charmingly laid back, sociable and 'green' place to stay. Go B&B, opt for the independence of self-catering, or bring your tent/camper van and pitch up under the almond, olive and fig trees. Décor is modest but attractive, some rooms have their own kitchens, others share. And you get acres of lovely untamed space. Make friends over dinner – the dining room, open during summer, serves tasty dishes from organic home produce, with plenty for vegetarians – or around the saltwater pool. Cafés, grocery stores and restaurants are just walkable (one mile), there's a daily bus to Lagos and wonderful clifftop walks on the south and west coasts; delightful Sandra and her relaxed staff know all the best spots and beaches. Massage and meditation, babysitting, riding and boat trips are bookable, there are bikes, billiards, books and games, hammocks and hens, pathways, terraces, barbecue areas and playground… families will be in heaven. *Minimum stay three nights.*

rooms	7 + 3: 5 twins/doubles, 1 single, 1 family. 3 houses for 4-8.
price	€45-€60. Singles €35-€45. Family room €60-€70. House €90-€125.
meals	Dinner with wine €15, April-November, 5 times a week. Restaurants nearby.
closed	Rarely.
directions	From Lagos for Aljezur; after 2km through Portelas; at end of village left to Barão. House 6km on left.

Sandra Falkena
tel   +351 282 687002
mobile   +351 918 552400
email   info@monterosaportugal.com
web   www.monterosaportugal.com

B&B & Self-catering

Map 5 Entry 155

Monte da Bravura
Cotifo, Caixa Polstal 1003 F, 8600-077 Bensafrim, Algarve

Could there be a more imaginative use of antiques? Tables and flower beds from old carts, an old trough for the cutlery and cloths, wall partitions from excavated local stone. This may be a modern house built from scratch 13 years ago, but it contains many stories – stories that retired Elisabete and Fernando are keen to share. Curious minds are encouraged and the inquisitive may stumble across a lesson in century-old traditional crop farming in the museum. The land itself was inherited from Elisabete's grandfather and draws many for winter-sun walks in the gorgeous Barragem. Given the house collection, the bedrooms and apartments are surprisingly uncluttered, with grand touches such as king-size beds, dressers and patchwork quilts adding colour to whitewash and terracotta. Heavy curtains keep rooms dark, but flick open to let in the distant glow of night-time lights over Lagos. Security and alarm systems abound. Garden-fresh vegetables complement tempting menus – served on white porcelain – for self-caterers escaping small but perfectly formed kitchenettes. *Minimum stay two nights.*

rooms	6 + 6 : 6 twins/doubles.
	6 apartments.
price	€70-€130.
meals	Lunch €20. Dinner €30.
closed	Rarely.
directions	On road between Vila de Odiaxere (5km) & Barragem de Bravura (2km).

Elisabete & Fernando Madeira

tel	+351 282 688175
fax	+351 282 687548
email	info@montedabravura.com
web	www.montedabravura.com

B&B & Self-catering

Map 5 Entry 156

Salsalito

Estrada da Luz, Burgau, 8600-146 Lagos, Algarve

A dream home that Ralph and Sally have spent some years creating. It's top-drawer 'Santa Fe' – all chunky beams, tree trunk shelves and quirky finds. The guest book tells it like it is: "perfect", "wonderful" and "award yourself 20 stars". Sally the designer loves funky chunky jewellery and Ralph is a master of all trades, including carpentry; his are the wardrobes, tables and door lintels. The sitting room has a huge log fire for cool nights and the bars – one on the top terrace – are brilliantly stocked. Sociable folk will love it here. Relax in summer in the horseshoe cloister with bamboo seats and wooden ceiling festooned with bougainvillea… then pad across to the lush pool, overlooked by a buddha and set among trees with a 'tropical' waterfall. The bedrooms have a touch of British B&B, with their kettles and teabags; one, in a converted outbuilding with a private terrace, is delightfully Mexican in style. You'll find masses to do: Burgau, with its bars and restaurants, two minutes by car, has kept something of its old fishing village character. *Minimum stay three nights. Children over 13 welcome.*

rooms	4: 3 doubles, 1 twin.
price	€75-€120 (€450-€750 per week).
meals	Restaurants in Burgau, 2km.
closed	November–March.
directions	A22 exit Lagos, to Vila do Bispo onto N125. Left at traffic lights for Almadena, then towards Burgau. At T-junc. over 1st speed bump, immed. right. If you reach the Pig's Head, you've gone too far.

	Ralph & Sally Eveleigh
tel/fax	+351 282 697628
mobile	+351 917 815751
email	salsalito@gmail.com
web	www.algarve-salsalito.com

B&B

Map 5 Entry 157

Quinta das Achadas

Estrada da Barragem, Odiáxere, 8600-251 Lagos, Algarve

Hats off to owners Júlio and Jill: their Quinta is one of the most convivial B&Bs of the Algarve. The approach is a delight, through groves of olive, almond and orange trees giving way to a subtropical garden where maguey and palm, geranium and bourgainvillea, pine and jasmine jostle for position. The living is easy here; there's a heated saltwater pool, a cabana with 'honesty' bar, a hydromassage jacuzzi and a small children's playground. The bedrooms, each with a small terrace, are in a converted barn and stables and overlook the gardens. They are Algarve-rustic, with wooden ceilings, white walls, modern art and beautiful country antiques. Shower rooms are lovely with Santa Katerina tiles. In colder weather you breakfast in a cosy dining room but most of the year it's mild enough to sit out on the rooftop terrace with views. The self-catering apartments are equally inviting, while dinners are three-course, eclectic and very good. Your hosts, who used to work in the restaurant trade, combine professionalism with a warm, human touch. Relaxing, and fun. *Minimum stay three nights in apartments.*

rooms	3 + 3: 3 twins/doubles. 3 apartments for 2-4.
price	€80-€110. Apartments €120-€180.
meals	Dinner with wine €25 (2-3 times a week).
closed	Rarely.
directions	From airport IP22 for Vilamoura & Portimão; exit 3. Straight over 1st r'bout; right for Odiaxere at 2nd r'bout. There, right at lights. Past windmill, bear left for Barragem; 1.3km on; house signed.

Jill, Júlio & Isabella Pires
tel   +351 282 798425
fax   +351 282 799162
email   info@algarveholiday.net
web   www.algarveholiday.net

B&B & Self-catering

Map 5 Entry 158

Quinta da Alfarrobeira

Estrada do Palmares, Odiáxere, 8600-252 Lagos, Algarve

For the young family from Holland, now embellishing their dream home, it was love at first sight. The 1730 farmhouse stands on a hill just inland from the Algarve coast and is surrounded by six hectares of old fruit groves. You might be fired by similar dreams as you sit beneath the enormous *alfarrobeira* (carob) and gaze out across the old olive and almond trees, or watch the family's three sons playing happily with their pets on a sunny flower-filled patio. Choose between the room in the main house, with own bathroom, and one of two guest houses renovated in traditional Algarve style where terracotta, beam and bamboo are the essential ingredients. We were impressed with their beautiful, light and airy feel and the antique furnishings that have been collected piecemeal from all over Europe. There are biggish bathrooms, private terraces and views – and little kitchens if you plan to cook. Add to this a hammock in the garden, a stylish pool, good walks from the door (less than a mile to the sea), exceptionally kind hosts and you may never want to leave. *Minimum stay three nights.*

rooms	1 + 2: 1 double. 2 houses: 1 for 2-4, 1 for 4-6.
price	€65-€85. Houses €65-€150 (€450-€1,050 per week).
meals	Restaurants 1.5km.
closed	Rarely.
directions	From Faro A22, then N125 towards Portimão & Lagos; exit Odiáxere. Left at square for Palmares. After 1.3km (cow sign on right), left. 1st house on right.

	Theo Bakker & Inge Keizer
tel	+351 282 798424
email	bakker@mail.telepac.pt

Casa da Palmeirinha

Rua da Igreja, 1, Mexilhoeira Grande, 8500-132 Portimão, Algarve

An old house, centred on its lush inner courtyard and garden that may remind you of houses of Seville or Morocco; it is also bigger than it seems. José, a local journalist who speaks English, was born here. The bedrooms have varied views of the church and village; the nicest open to a terrace and roof garden with views of the Alvor bird sanctuary. The Spanish-influenced sitting room has walls decorated with flamboyant tiles, a gleaming terracotta floor and a rustic feel. Then there's that huge courtyard with its ornamental pool, swimming pool and lawn, shaded by arching palms – a cool and peaceful place to relax, sometimes shared by the owner's Algarve water dogs and labrador. This is an unusual opportunity to stay in a Portuguese townhouse that is attractive inside and out, but it is true to say you are very much left to your own devices (and you are free to make tea and coffee in the kitchen). The village is genuine, full of locals with the bonus of the famous Vila Lisa restaurant. There's a bird sanctuary nearby, and good walks.
Minimum stay two nights.

rooms	5: 3 doubles, 2 family rooms.
price	€60-€80. Singles €50-€60. Family rooms €77-€97.
meals	Restaurants nearby.
closed	December.
directions	From Portimão or Lagos on N125; into Mexilhoeira Grande to church. House on left, turn left.

	Senhor José Manuel Júdice Glória
tel	+351 282 969277
mobile	+351 917 546502
fax	+351 282 180714
email	josejudice@mail.telepac.pt

B&B

Map 5 Entry 160

Casa Três Palmeiras
Apartado 84, 8501-909 Portimão, Algarve

What a setting! From the Casa's perch by the cliff edge the view is a symphony of
rock, sea and sky — ever-changing according to the day's mood, ever beautiful.
The villa was built in the Sixties when the Algarve was discovered, and the mood
is luxurious zen... all you hear are seagulls and waves. Simple white arches and
three tall palms (*três palmeiras*) soften the façade and give welcome shade once the
temperature rises. Bedrooms have everything you might expect for the price —
polished floors, walk-in wardrobes, generous beds and bathrooms lavishly tiled; all
is beautifully uncluttered. Four lead directly onto a parasoled terrace with
heavenly views and saltwater pool. It is a supremely comfortable house full of
fruit and flowers, and a woodburner for winter cosiness. The service is warm yet
professional: kind Dolly, from Brazil, makes everything perfect, from massage to
pedicure. A path leads from the house down to the beach; breakfast early and you
may find you have it all to yourself, even in midsummer. Book ahead for high
summer. *Reduced green fees & car hire rates.*

rooms	5 twins/doubles.
price	€155–€185.
meals	Breakfast not included.
	Snacks available for lunch.
closed	December–January.
directions	From Portimão, dual carriageway for Praia da Rocha. Right at last r'bout for Praia do Vau; at next r'bout, double back & turn up track on right after 100m. Right along track at 1st villa.

	Dolly Schlingensiepen
tel	+351 282 401275
fax	+351 282 401029
email	dolly@casatrespalmeiras.com
web	www.casatrespalmeiras.com

B&B

Map 5 Entry 161

Rio Arade

Rua D.Joáo II 33, Mexilhoeira da Carregacáo, 8400-092 Estombar, Algarve

Wrought-iron balconies, colourful window mouldings and gleaming beamed ceilings – this is every inch the handsome Portuguese townhouse. To find it amongst the hurly-burly of the Algarve coast is a treat. The 18th-century house in this former fishing village has been smartly modernised: step in to a cool, light space and a honey-coloured floor studded with creamy sofas. Behind is the dining area, traditional with rush-seated ladderback chairs and bright yellow china; beyond, the courtyard with its brilliant blue pool, terraces and shady corners. Very peaceful, very Portuguese – bougainvillea, palms, fountains and sufficient space to tuck yourself away from other guests. Sunny bedrooms are comfortable and uncluttered with breezy colour themes. Some rooms have rugs on polished wooden floors, others have creamy ceramic tiles, the best have private terraces overlooking the pool. Free use of the swish leisure spa nearby is a big plus. John, affable Irishman and retired marathon runner, might join you. He'll also point you in the direction of the village's best restaurants. *Minimum stay three nights.*

rooms	9: 3 doubles, 6 twins.
price	€55–€110.
meals	Restaurants nearby.
closed	Rarely.
directions	From Faro, A22 signed 'West/Portimao'; exit 6, signs to Lagoa/Silves; 3rd exit at r'bout for Estombar; signs to Estombar, right at lights; 200m, house on left.

	John O'Neill
tel	+351 282 423202
mobile	+351 969 459029
email	info@rioarade.com
web	www.rioarade.com

Guest house

Map 5 Entry 162

Na Curva do Rio
Caixa Postal 2259, 8400-066 Estombar/Lagoa, Algarve

Here, high above the river Arade, you can watch the bizarre sight of seagulls cavorting in the olive trees. The salt pans opposite attract all sorts of birds – residents and migrants. (You would barely know you were three kilometres from the motorway – there's just a distant hum.) In the rambling old farmhouse, rooms are a luminous mix of white and bright colours, enhanced by painted furniture and Lourenços' mother's paintings. Add old stone troughs for sinks, painted wrought-iron beds, fluttering muslin curtains and woodburning stoves in rooms for winter stays and you have a small guest house that is stylishly rustic. There's a big funky sitting room with squashy sofas for lounging in; for summer, shady terraces and a pool. There's masses to do; set off for the day and you could find yourself canoeing, fishing, sailing, playing golf or swimming in a tributary of the river in the park nearby. They also provide a boat taxi service and can drop you off at a deserted beach with a picnic. The whole place has a youthful feel and your hosts Lourenço, and Brazilian Elsa, who cooks, are charming.

rooms	8 doubles.
price	€100–€130. Full & half-board prices available.
meals	Lunch & dinner from €17.50, on request.
closed	Rarely.
directions	Directions on booking.

Senhor Lourenço Ribeiro
tel +351 282 482125
fax +351 282 482125
email nacurvadorio@mail.telepac.pt
web www.nacurvadorio.com

Guest house

Map 5 Entry 163

Vila Domilu

Estrada de Benagil, Alfanzina, 8401-910 Carvoeiro, Algarve

This small resort-hotel under new ownership flaunts its frills at every turn. If neo-Doric columns and musak are not your thing, keep away… But if you long to stay in a glitzy place to stay on the Algarve, come here! The décor of lounge and dining room is pick-and-mix: repro antiques, Art Deco-style chairs, glass-topped tables, dragon-tooth floors. Most bedrooms are big, light, cheerful and marble-floored and have all the extras; book the honeymoon suite and you get a sunken whirlpool bath surrounded by potted palms. Outside, sweeping colonnaded steps lead to a fabulous new palm-studded terrace with curvaceous pool and children's pool; newer bedrooms, too. The saltwater indoor pool, with jacuzzi, is equally gorgeous. Breakfast is buffet, big and designed to please northern European palates – many guests are German – while candlelit dinner is resolutely Portuguese. There is tennis (floodlit at night) a gymnasium, sauna and beauty spa, and mountain bikes; beaches and golf courses are a saunter away. Staff are delightful and many guests return.

rooms	42 twins/doubles/suites.
price	€60–€214. Suites €120–€440.
meals	Dinner, 3 courses, €30–€40.
closed	Rarely.
directions	From N125, exit for Carvoeiro. 200m after Intermarché supermarket, left at signs for house.

	Paulo Bica
tel	+351 282 350610
fax	+351 282 358410
email	central@viladomilu.com
web	www.viladomilu.com

Hotel

Map 5 Entry 164

Casa Bela Moura

Estrada de Porches 530, Alporchinhos, 8400-450 Porches, Algarve

The welcome is exceptional and Christophe and Sofie are Belgian and fired up with enthusiasm for their venture. This is a small, charming villa-hotel, set well back from the road, three minutes from the pretty beach of Senhora da Rocha where you'll find a little chapel. Breakfasts are lavish and change every day: ham, cereal, yogurt, fresh pineapple, just-squeezed orange juice, four different types of bread, scrambled eggs, French toast… and there are coffee and cakes in the afternoon. After a lazy day by the pool, retire to the cosy lounge for a summery aperitif – or a nightcap before the fire; this is where plans are made, often with the help of fellow guests, for tomorrow's excursions. Visit Lagos, Silves, the Serra de Monchique, the old centre of Faro – you are perfectly sited for all. Cheery bedrooms are in the main villa (they also have five family rooms which are let privately to a tour operator). Some rooms have terraces, three have baths (some modern and snazzy), the rest showers, and the suite, with its 'rain' shower, is an absolute treat. *Minimum stay two nights.*

rooms	8: 2 doubles, 5 twins, 1 suite.
price	€75-€180. Singles €35-€105.
meals	Light lunch €2-€5. Half-board deal with good local restaurant.
closed	January.
directions	From Faro A22, exit 7 Alcantarilha. At r'bout, N125 to Portimão. After 3km, left in Porches for Armação de Pera. House on right after 3km, before Cespa petrol station.

	Christophe Rijnders & Sofie Blyaert
tel	+351 282 313422
fax	+351 282 313025
email	casabelamoura@sapo.pt
web	www.casabelamoura.com

Hotel

Map 5 Entry 165

Casa das Oliveiras

Montes da Vala, 8300-044 Silves, Algarve

Off the dusty beaten track, surrounded by fruit and olive trees and with an English welcome of homemade cake and tea, here is an unassuming, family-run guest house – no more, no less. It is an affordable and friendly place from which to explore this pretty part of Portugal. You have quiet beaches 15 minutes away, walking and cycling along the coast (and in the hills around Monchique), Silves with its castle and cathedral and seafood suppers above Portimão's harbour. Bill and Isa are charming and helpful but never intrusive. Their modern home is spotless and traditionally furnished without fuss or frills, a touch dated but never less than comfortable. Simple bedrooms have high ceilings, wooden furniture and tiled floors, and open to the pool terrace or garden. One has its own private patio. Guests come and go as they please; to shady spots around the pool and garden or, on chillier days, to a wood-burning stove in the breakfast room. And there's a small kitchen corner so you rustle up a simple meal: excellent for families. The motorway is in sight but all you hear here is the rustling of the trees.

rooms	5: 2 doubles, 3 twins. Cots & extra beds available.
price	€40-€60.
meals	Restaurants 4-6km.
closed	Rarely.
directions	A22 exit 7 for Alcantarilha. Leave r'bout at 1st exit towards Silves; 3km, left towards Lagoa; 4km, right just before viaduct; follow signs.

	Bill & Isa Reed
tel	+351 282 342115
mobile	+351 963 136938
email	contact@casa-das-oliveiras.com
web	www.casa-das-oliveiras.com

Guest house

Map 5 Entry 166

Quinta Dimalago
Sitio Canine, 8300-022 Silves, Algarve

Silves is the oldest city in the Algarve and Quinta Dimalago has a fantastic view of its Moorish castle – gorgeous when floodlit at night. Great swathes of open countryside unfurl before you – and that's just the start of Utopia. The big, beautiful, tropical garden with its natural pool and waterfalls is on a migrating path for birds and is a wildlife haven. Then there are two pools (one for each house), a sauna, a jacuzzi, an outdoor wok kitchen and a playground for kids. Choose between the renovated 200-year cottage – stunning with its Sri Lankan doors, Dutch antiques and Moroccan suite – and the newly-built quinta, whose modest shell hides a strikingly decorated and superbly well furnished and equipped interior. Though the kitchen should make self-catering a delight, there is a chef on call should you wish to be spoiled. Generous rooms have natural ventilation, while solar panels and rainwater harvesting reflect the green consciences of these relaxed and delightful Dutch owners. They live opposite and welcome you on arrival with a glass of sparkling wine. Heaven. *Minimum stay one week.*

rooms	Cottage for 4. House for 12.
price	€595–€1,950 per week.
meals	Self-catering. Restaurants 10-minute walk.
closed	Rarely.
directions	Between Silves & Messines, follow signs for Cruz Portugal; turn onto old Road of San Marcos de Sierra. Left after river, at windmill.

	Arnold Aarssen
tel	+351 282 4457760
mobile	+351 962 042933
email	arnoldaarssen@sapo.pt
web	dimalago.spaces.live.com/

Self-catering

Map 5 Entry 167

Quinta do Caçapo
Franqueira 402/L, 8300-019 Silves, Algarve

Gerry and Dolf came to Portugal on the eve of the Carnation Revolution in 1974 – and stayed. Now they live in this lovely yellow farmhouse, on a gentle ridge above the Algarve coast. It's a peaceful spot, with only the quacking of the neighbours' ducks to break the silence – and the odd splash from the pool. Lovely big bedrooms have terracotta floors, chunky furniture and original art, super bathrooms in blue or green, and French windows opening to a veranda for breakfast. Which is a good and generous spread, and includes homemade jams from the fig, orange and apricot trees. The Algarvian garden is lush with yuccas, palms, oleanders and almond trees; views stretch to the mountains of Monchique. Next to the terrace is a pretty bread oven topped by a ceramic rabbit – *caçapo* means bunny and was the nickname of the previous owner. Just 15 kilometres from the coast and eight from Silves, the ancient Moorish capital of the Algarve, this is fantastic value. Your hosts speak four languages between them and couldn't be nicer. *25% discount in winter.*

rooms	3 twins/doubles.
price	€65–€73.50 (€445 per week).
meals	Light lunch on request.
closed	Never.
directions	Faro A22 dir. Portimão; exit 8. Left towards Pera, immed. right onto road for Monte Raposo, 2.5km; right at T-junc.; on for 4.3km. Right at railway line; immed. left over line; thro' Fonte Louseiros, right at sign after Reino das Pedras restaurant; 400m on right.

	Gerry Atkins
tel	+351 282 332747
fax	+351 282 332747
email	cacapo@sapo.pt
web	www.cacapo.cjb.net

B&B

Map 5 Entry 168

Monte das Cortelhas
Caminho do Monte, 8200-413 Guia, Algarve

These are the nicest hosts: warm and gracious, helpful and kind. Off the N125, past the cork oaks, down the half-mile drive and you enter another world; open countryside and only the faintest motorway hum. There's a mix of B&B rooms and one self-catering apartment at the whitewashed 1840 farmstead, the décor is pleasingly simple, typically Portuguese, and the gardens are gorgeous and cared for. Terraces are roofed with straw, jasmine drifts on the breeze, the fountains play, there's birdsong to wake you and cicada-strum at night. Breakfast is served in the dining room with saffron walls and is fully organic, the fruit straight from the trees. Bedrooms have chunky rafters and pure white walls, firm new beds, rustic terracotta floors and views onto orchards or fields. Showers have soft white towels. The pool is a step away, quaint little Guia, full of lovely restaurants, is a shortish walk. With a remote control on the security gate you can come and go as you please and there's a big welcome for families. *Minimum stay two nights in apartment.*

rooms	4 + 1: 4 doubles. 1 apartment for 4.
price	€80. Apartment €600 per week.
meals	Restaurants 500m.
closed	December.
directions	At r'bout in Guia, take Portimão turning. House 500m on right.

Senhor António Silvestre
tel/fax +351 289 561487
mobile +351 912 115472
email montecortelhas@iol.pt
web www.montecortelhas.com

B&B & Self-catering

Map 5 Entry 169

Quinta da Cebola Vermelha
Campina, PO Box 141, 8100-908 Boliqueime, Algarve

So pristine one wonders how the old farmhouse can have so much personality – but it has. The owners are special too: cultured, stylish and friendly, adept at combining ancient and modern yet quite capable of witty and imaginative flourishes. (Paintings by 'new' Portuguese artists are high on their list for the future.) Much of the mood is Moroccan – but not at the hippy end of the spectrum! Bedrooms sparkle with colour, generosity and space, there are big quarry tiles and pale, plain walls. The taste is refreshing, and impeccable. The roomy beds are singles side by side, the bathrooms are vast and gorgeous. The swimming pool, too, is huge, set about with straw parasols and smart recliners, and a tabled lawn fragrant with orange trees to one side – bliss for a lunchtime snack. There are also some very gnarled and magnificent old olive trees. The food is the best of home cooking, the sea is 15 minutes by car, and the Algarve's hustle is safely out of reach. Let our inspector have the last word: "I defy anyone not to like it here: it is utterly gorgeous."

rooms	6 doubles/twins.
price	€95-€105. Singles €85. Extra bed €25.
meals	Restaurant 1km.
closed	Mid-December-January.
directions	From Faro A22 for Albufeira, exit Boliqueme. At r'bout into village; straight on, then right for Picota & Alfontes. Right; at sign to Campina, right again. Continue to house.

Ard, Noor & Bastiaan Yssel de Schepper

tel	+351 289 363680
fax	+351 289 363688
email	info@quintadacebolavermelha.com
web	www.quintadacebolavermelha.com

B&B

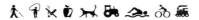

Map 5 Entry 170

The Garden Cottages

North of Vilamoura, 8100-292 Loulé, Algarve

In a lush valley a couple of miles back from the coast, long hours of sunshine and rich soil allow nearly everything to grow in profusion. The English owner found this old wine farm in ruins in the early 70s and put in a fair bit of patient restoration and planting. This is a place of peace and privacy; behind the whitewashed outer wall the cottages stand apart from one another facing the gardens and, tucked away beyond, is an enormous round swimming pool known as 'the library'... such is the peace. Each cottage has a sun and a shade terrace, a tiled kitchen, a sitting room and double or twin bedroom with a shower – just right for two. A mix of good art and 'jumble sale' finds, pretty dried flowers, eucalyptus beams and terracotta give a country feel, while mementos from Africa and Turkey add an exotic note. But what is most striking is the greenery: olive, pomegranate, almond and lemon trees flourish in the gardens and, beneath, profusions of flowers. A local shop and three restaurants are within walking distance, and the climate is benign all year.

rooms	6 cottages for 2.
price	£200-£400 per week.
meals	Self-catering. Restaurants within walking distance.
closed	Never.
directions	Directions on booking.

Debbie Boyes

tel	+44 (0)1462 817377
fax	+44 (0)1462 817377
email	debbie@rmlboyes.fsnet.co.uk
web	www.algarvegardencottage.co.uk

Self-catering

Map 5 Entry 171

Quintassential Holiday Cottages

Apartado 1161, 8101-904 Loulé, Algarve

The road is steep, but the views spilling over the Atlantic will take your breath away – blue, sparkling, unbroken. This old Portuguese farmhouse and its outbuildings have been sensitively converted and extended. Rooms have a rustic, modern simplicity: solid wood furniture, pretty tiles, embroidered cushions, colourful pottery. There are woodburning stoves and microwaves, shelves of books, private terraces and barbecues – sophisticated yet cosy. For complete privacy, choose Casa do Forno, the converted bread oven; tiny, gorgeous, intimate, it is the ultimate in ergonomic design. Although temptingly near lively beaches and Loulé town, it's hard to drag yourself away from those views: the roof terrace has a horizon-wide panorama from the foothills of Monchique all the way to the Algarve coast. A terraced garden, swimming pool and shady patio bar – you can dine here once a week in summer on well-priced, traditional dishes – add to the choice of places to linger. Rosa (Portuguese) and Mike (English) are friendly without being intrusive. Great for a couple – or a big party. *Minimum stay three nights.*

rooms	4 cottages for 2-4 (max. 13 people).
price	£310-£825 per week.
meals	Self-catering.
	Restaurants 2-minute drive.
closed	Rarely.
directions	From airport to Loulé. From Loulé north on Salir road for two minutes. Detailed directions on booking.

Rosa Gulliver

tel	+351 289 463867
email	info@quintassential.com
web	www.quintassential.com

Casa Borboleta

5 Clemente, Carvalho, 8100-235 Loulé, Algarve

At last, somewhere to bring the young ones and not worry about messing up the furniture. Two self-catering cottages each house four comfortably and in some style. It's quiet too, a secret of deepest darkest Portugal; rumour has it that the original house was once the village shop. There's a great garden with a play area for children and a pool that bobs with inflatables. Enjoy a barbecue lunch on the patio with plenty of chairs, tables and merciful shade. There are shared washing facilities and a load of DVDs in the 'Donkey House'. Sitting rooms are large, informal affairs with throws on the furniture adding colour to simple walls and stone floors. Good-sized kitchens are well-equipped to feed the hungry, although Nikki provides a generous welcome pack, including two bottles of wine and a good joint of beef. She can also deliver homemade dinners at reasonable prices. Guests are encouraged to recycle and respect water, including dousing the plants with used water from the sink. And pretty Querença village offers house chefs a gourmet break.

rooms	2 cottages for 4–6.
price	From £380 per week.
meals	Self-catering. Restaurant 2km.
closed	Rarely.
directions	From airport to Loulé. After 3rd r'bout (dual c'way becomes single lane), 1st right opp. garage. Up left to bandstand; straight on; over 3 r'bouts onto Querença Rd; cont. to Clareanes; 1st right to Carvalho; 1 mile; on right.

	Nick & Nikky Bartlett
tel	+44 (0)1252 703613
fax	+44 (0)1252 706844
email	info@casaborboleta.com
web	www.casaborboleta.com

Self-catering

Map 6 Entry 173

Casa Charneca

Sitio da Charneca 502A, 8005-440 Santa Barbara de Nexe, Faro, Algarve

A sanctuary above the Algarve, yet only 15 minutes from dazzling white beaches. This stylish villa, in the hills of Santa Barbara, combines privacy with idiosyncratic touches. Modern lighting, French antiques, contemporary sofas and 19th- and 20th-century art rub shoulders delightfully. Ronny and Thierry, an engaging and gentle couple, know how to spoil and give a big welcome to gay and straight guests. White bedrooms are understatedly comfortable with large beds, clubby armchairs and rich fabrics; a Casablanca fan, Art Nouveau lampshade or splash of art add an exotic feel. The secluded smaller bedroom by the fish-shaped, dolphin-mosaic pool is a favourite with single guests. Breakfasts and dinners (the latter generally on Mondays, Tuesdays and Fridays) have a French flavour and are dictated by the day's markets. After a mouthwatering mousse au chocolat or tiramisu, work off the calories in the small gym, sauna and jacuzzi. For easy-going, open-minded grown-ups it's refreshing and fun. Views stretch for miles, the peace is total. *Minimum stay three nights.*

rooms	4 doubles.
price	€75–€120. Singles from €55.
meals	Dinner 3 days a week. Restaurants S. Barbara de Nexe, 10-minute drive.
closed	Rarely.
directions	At S. Barbara Church head towards S. Bras for 2km; right at Casa Crow. House at very end of track.

	Ronny & Thierry Soenen
tel	+351 289 992842
mobile	+351 965 402474
email	casacharneca@hotmail.com
web	www.casacharneca.com

B&B

Map 6 Entry 174

Casa da Calma

Sitio de Pereiro, CX Postal 327x, 8700-123 Moncarapacho, Algarve

Pick your own oranges for breakfast! Nicole's hotel in the unspoiled hills is surrounded by verdant gardens and lawns. Hospitality runs in the family: German-born Nicole worked in the tourist industry for years; her mother, chief cook, ran a guest house in California. Décor at the renovated 1940s farmhouse is hotel-comfortable but not anonymous and each room is different: matching paisley bedcovers and curtains in one, Portuguese beds in another. All have their own generous terraces, fluffy white bathrobes, poolside towels and bowls of fruit. Buffet breakfasts are a spread, the honesty bar is well-stocked, dinner may include fish. The heated pool is decked with loungers and jolly parasols, there's a sauna to spoil you and a massage on request. Never mind the closeness of the road; you are conveniently placed for the lovely island beaches of Armona and Tavira, and your hostess is an expert when it comes to trips: riding, sailing, waterskiing, fishing, golf. She also organizes shopping trips to charming Lisbon – or over the border to Seville. *Minimum stay four nights July-Sept.*

rooms	6: 4 twins/doubles, 1 family suite, 1 suite.
price	€80-€138. Singles €55-€75. Suite €140-€200.
meals	Dinner €15-€20, by arrangement.
closed	Never.
directions	Faro A22 for Spain. Exit 15 Olhão & Moncarapacho. On towards Sta Catarina. House on left after 2km.

	Nicole Effenberg
mobile	+351 914 798187
fax	+351 289 791599
email	info@casadacalma.com
web	www.casadacalma.com

Hotel

Map 6 Entry 175

Monte do Casal
Cerro do Lobo, Estoi, 8005-436 Faro, Algarve

Breakfast on your terrace, take afternoon tea round the pool, dine above a
magically lit garden. It has taken Bill Hawkins 20 years to get this 18th-century
manor house, high above the Algarve, to his liking. It is luxurious but not grand,
smart but easy. The colonial-style drawing room has padded sofas, piles of books,
beautiful flowers. Bedrooms – some in a separate villa a short walk away – are
large but homely in understated country-house style: polished mahogany, pastel
walls, watercolours, books and a choice of pillows! Some overlook the gardens,
others have views to the sea. There are special touches everywhere: flowers, CD
players, books, internet access and sunloungers on each private terrace. The
Waterfall Villa spoils with a garden *and* a waterfall. When you tire of the
swimming pools and whirlpools (two of each), explore the gardens, fountains and
rockpools, rich with scent and colour. Dine – gourmand? Thai? classic Algarve?
you choose – accompanied by candles and open fires; in summer under the
pergola. A relaxing place for grown-ups, with a fine welcome.

rooms	18: 12 twins/doubles.
	Villa: 6 twins/doubles.
price	€130-€400.
meals	Lunch €15. Dinner €29.
	Menu 'gourmand', 5 courses, €50.
closed	26 November-13 December;
	4 January-12 February.
directions	In Estoi, at square, turn towards
	Moncarapacho; hotel 2.5km along
	road, signed on left.

	Bill Hawkins
tel	+351 289 991503
fax	+351 289 991341
email	montecasal@mail.telepac.pt
web	www.montedocasal.pt

Hotel

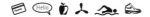

Map 6 Entry 176

Pedras Verdes Guesthouse

Sítio da Boavista, CP 658 T Quelfes, 8700 Olhão, Algarve

The house is low and north-African style, surrounded by carob and olive trees.
The bedrooms are all different, all special: baroque, African, Asiatic, Arabic, zen.
Expect a minimalist décor: funky walk-in showers with pebbled or wooden
flooring, plain walls, Portuguese antiques and modern pieces. The Asiatic room
has fresh palms, exquisite bedcovers and ceiling nets over the bed. Little touches
make an impact – artistically placed fruit in the bedrooms, sweets, fresh flowers,
postcards – while each key has a symbol: a cowrie shell for the Asiatic room,
an ebony sculpted head for the African. The humour in the décor reflects the
character of the lovely owners – Muriel and André are charming, welcoming and
enthusiastic about creating beautiful spaces. The stylish feel extends to the garden
where stone sculptures are filled with exotic shells and crystals. Relax by the
serene seawater pool or under the canvas canopy and let the peacefulness wash
over you. There's opera at breakfast, delicious dinner is served on a beautiful
wooden table, and the cocktails are sublime. Oh, and there's a sweet dog.

rooms	6 twins/doubles.
price	€75-€95.
meals	Dinner €18-€22 (Fridays only).
closed	Mid-November-mid-February.
directions	From Faro airport N125-10 to São Brás; on to N2, then A22 to Spain; exit 15 Olhão 'Quelfes'. Enter village, sharp left-hand bend at white building with red base; sharp right, follow green stones. Tricky to find at night.

	André & Muriel Mandi
tel	+351 289 721343
fax	+351 289 721343
email	info@pedrasverdes.com
web	www.pedrasverdes.com

B&B

Map 6 Entry 177

Estalagem Quinta Jacintina

32/33 Urb. Quinta Jacintina, Apartado 3326, 8135-025 Garrâo, Algarve

Everything here is immaculate, from the Italian fresco on the walls to the bathroom soaps. It's a labour of love for Brian and Monica (an interior designer) – they're perfectionists and it shows. Take the to-die-for Egyptian cotton sheets, and the way breakfast (croissants, palmiers, homemade rolls) is set out on your private patio ready for your waking. Your hosts live nearby but keep an eagle eye on everything to make sure it's just-so, and their loving attention to detail has rubbed off on their staff, who are attentive and welcoming. The design is luxurious-traditional, with whites and pale hues spectacularly shot through with colour. Pinks, reds and greens flare like beacons against cream walls in the restaurant where Mediterranean food is served – and the grounds are exquisitely landscaped, showing the talents of the couple's son. This is an upmarket hotel in an area that has everything, from Blue Flag beaches to golf, *and* the Rio Formosa nature reserve. French windows and private balconies, mini bars and drinks served by the pool, very welcoming owners... all you need for a stupendous stay.

rooms	11: 10 doubles, 1 suite.
price	€220–€360.
meals	€40–€50.
closed	December–February.
directions	From m'way exit 12 towards Quarteira to Quatro Estradas traffic lights. Left onto N125, down hill, take slip road on right for Almancil. 1st right signed; at staggered junction almost straight across; cont. around bends; 1st on left.

Brian & Monica Pullin

tel	+351 289 350090
fax	+351 289 350099
email	info@algarvehotel.co.uk
web	www.algarvehotel.co.uk

Hotel

Map 6 Entry 178

Quinta da Ra

Sitio do Arroio, Luz de Tavira, 8800-101 Tavira, Algarve

Come for peace and comfort in great measure, and grounds that are a joy to explore. Carob, almond, olive, pomegranate, lemon – all grow in profusion. The swimming pool is huge and the cabana ideal for barbecues sheltered from the sun. The spacious, Moorish-style house has been built around a central courtyard and is a luxurious mix of modern and traditional: wooden vaulted ceilings, a state-of-the-art kitchen, a spectacular Italian woodburning range, a dining table that converts into a table for pool. Comfortable beds have wrought-iron bedheads; quarry floors are heated for winter; fitted cupboards have solid carved doors. Sink into a tan leather sofa for a spot of satellite TV; drift outside, find a shady terrace and a wicker armchair, pluck a few grapes, nod off by the fountain… you'd be hard-pushed not to unwind at the Quinta da Ra. For shops and cafés there's Tavira, 'jewel of the Algarve', the Rio Formosa Reserve is amazing for birds, and Seville is a day trip away. Dave and Rhona, who manage the Quinta for the owners, live close by and are a fund of local knowledge.

rooms	House for 6 (2 doubles, 1 twin).
price	€1,499-€2,499 per week.
meals	Self-catering. Restaurants 2km.
closed	Rarely.
directions	Faro airport dir. Tavira; 7km Luz de Tavira. Right, opp. green-tiled house (Estrada das Antas); 250m on, cross railway; immed. right; left in front of two houses; left after 125m; right at T-junc. Signed on left after No Through Road.

	Joyce Boor
tel	+44 (0)1651 863149
email	jboor@toucansurf.com
web	www.quintadara.co.uk

Quinta da Lua

Bernardinheiro 1622-X, S. Estevão, 8800-513 Tavira, Algarve

Staying at the 'Farm of the Moon' is delightful on many levels. Miguel and Vimal have stacks of enthusiasm, love looking after people and the food is especially good; don't miss Vimal's once-weekly dinners. Breakfast, served on the wooden terrace, is different every day, and guests are asked their preferences. The house, surrounded by orange trees and vineyards, carob, oleander, bougainvillea and palms, is a two-storey addition to an old Algarve farmhouse, and there's a lovely saltwater pool in the well-groomed gardens — with shaded verandas to the side, and an 'honesty' fridge/bar for drinks. Inside: a stylish blend of modern and traditional, with rustic terracotta tiles and beamed ceilings throughout. Bedrooms are perfect: simple but luxurious; beds are generous, the soundproofing is good and the suites are huge. The moon logo is duplicated in two colours in the bath and shower rooms — you won't borrow your room mate's towel by mistake! Not one for families, but a surprise to find such a special place so close to the island beaches and the restaurants of Tavira, run by such nice people.

rooms	8: 6 twins/doubles, 2 suites.
price	€65-€120. Suites €100-€150.
meals	Lunch €17.
	Dinner €25 (once a week).
closed	Never.
directions	From Faro, A22 to Spain, exit Tavira. At 2nd r'bout, N125 for Olhão. Right to S. Estevão. 1st left; at next right, look for arch over Quinta gateway.

Miguel Martins & Vimal Willems

tel	+351 281 961070
fax	+351 281 961070
email	quintadalua@quintadalua.com.pt
web	www.quintadalua.com.pt

Guest house

Map 6 Entry 180

Quinta da Fonte Bispo

Estrada National 270, Cx. Postal 797-A, Fonte do Bispo, 8800-161 Tavira, Algarve

Enjoy the benign climate, exceptional vegetation and closeness to the sea in the gentle hills of the Algarve hinterland. This old farmstead will inspire affection for the region, and it is run by the kindest people. It is a long, low, white building with pretty chimney stacks and broad bands of blue around doors and windows – near the road but peaceful. Parts of the farm are 200 years old but it has been completely renovated. The six suites in the converted outbuildings, fronting a cobbled central patio, were designed with families in mind: open-plan sitting rooms have beds which double up as sofas and open fires for cosy winter days. The style is local and 'country': herringbone terracotta floors, beamed and bamboo roofs, simple yet adequate shower rooms. There is a large communal sitting room in similar style but most of the year you will be out by the pool; find a shady spot beneath the orange, almond or olive trees. The restaurant serves Portuguese food (delicious cheeses and chorizo), and there are a sauna, table-tennis, pool and mini-gym. *Minimum stay two nights. Painting courses available.*

rooms	6 suites for 4. Extra beds available.
price	€65-€95.
meals	Lunch €17.50. Dinner €20.
closed	Rarely.
directions	From Faro, A22 for Spain. Exit 15 for Santa Catarina; right for Tavira; Quinta signed on left after 1km.

Senhora Helena Brito Neto

tel	+351 281 971484
fax	+351 281 971714
email	info@qtfontebispo.com
web	www.qtfontebispo.com

B&B

Map 6 Entry 181

Casa Vale del Rei
Almargem, 8800-053 Tavira, Algarve

Robin and Geraldine fell in love with their holiday guest house and came back to buy it. You can see why. Perched on a hilltop close – but not too close – to the cobbled fishing town of Tavira, this handsome, whitewashed villa is surrounded by orange and olive groves and sweeping views of the coastline. Cabanas beach is a five-minute drive, three golf courses lie not much further. Not that you will want to leave in a hurry; Casa Vale del Rei is heaven in summer with its waterlily ponds, fountains and shady corners, its oleander, lavender, palms, pines and lazy pool. Your friendly, helpful hosts have created a stylish and contemporary interior without spoiling the authentic Algarve feel. Bathrooms are glistening white, bedrooms cool and lofty with natural materials: muslin curtains, white-painted furniture, pretty cotton fabrics. Breakfast and sitting rooms are similarly spare, in cool creams and taupes, with stylish splashes from chandeliers, antiqued mirrors and vibrant fabric pictures. If it's warm, breakfast under the old alfarabos tree. After dinner, return to the peace of your hideaway.

rooms	7: 2 doubles, 3 twins, 2 family rooms.
price	€55–€90.
meals	Restaurant 150m.
closed	Rarely.
directions	From Faro A22 E for Spain, exit 16 Tavira. At 2nd r'bout, N125 for Vila Real. Pass Eurotel on left, left at sign to Almargem. Left up track after white bridge on right.

Robin Ford-Jones

tel	+351 281 323099
fax	+351 281 323099
email	casavaledelrei@hotmail.com
web	www.casavaledelrei.co.uk

Guest house

Map 6 Entry 182

The Tavira Inn
Rua Chefe António Afonso, 39, 8800-251 Tavira, Algarve

Warm and witty, fun and funky; if a guest house can reflect its owner, the Tavira Inn surely does. Sebastião Bastos, a man of middle years and relaxed good humour, has combined his love of travel, music and art with his background in hotel management to create an off-beat but deliciously relaxing Special Place. Close to the centre of Tavira and overlooking the river, the townhouse combines old with new: tiled floors and Portuguese fireplaces with bold art and bright chairs. The seawater pool and terrace hide beneath a railway bridge — passing trains, oddly, add to the fun. The five guest rooms, double-glazed and very quiet, are colourfully and eclectically furnished — perhaps an antique wardrobe, a quilted bedspread, an exotically patterned rug, a Moroccan ceramic. Bathrooms are cool and modern with prettily tiled mirrors. The bar is the centre of activity, full of huge umbrellas and good humour. Laze by the pool, stroll into Tavira (three minutes), catch the boat to the beach. Come evening, relax to soul, jazz or gentle music around the bar. You'll probably decide to stay another day.

rooms	5 doubles.
price	€65–€130.
meals	Restaurant 200m.
closed	November–January.
directions	From motorway, follow signs for Tavira. House below bridge on N125 next to river. Follow signs for Tavira; take junction for Ponte Ferroviária.

Senhor Sebastião Bastos
tel/fax	+351 281 326578
mobile	+351 917 356623
email	booking@tavira-inn.com
web	www.tavira-inn.com

B&B

Map 6 Entry 183

Convento de Santo António
Rua de Santo António 56, 8800-705 Tavira, Algarve

What a surprise! An inauspicious area, but seek out a tiny door in the ancient wooden gate by the chapel… it leads, incredibly, to this dazzling white convent surrounded by lush vegetation and circular pool. Isabel is almost apologetic that "the home has only been in the family for five generations". A portrait of great-grandmother gazes down one of the vaulted corridors that runs the length of the 17th-century cloister while Santo António looks on benignly from his chapel. The whole place is a Lusitanian feast of hand-crafted terracotta, flowered and striped *alcobaça* fabrics and carefully chosen, often naïve, paintings. The bedrooms vary in size and have a convent-like charm: here a vaulted ceiling, there a fine dresser. We loved the lofty Chapel Room for honeymooners, its bathroom sitting snugly inside what was a chimney breast. Sitting room and bar are just as special and entirely candlelit at night – as peaceful as when the Capuchin monks dwelt here. You are near the historic centre of Tavira, yet a short walk from the beach. Gracious and special. *Minimum stay three to five nights.*

rooms	5: 4 twins/doubles, 1 suite.
price	€120-€180. Suite €200-€250.
meals	Restaurants within walking distance.
closed	Never.
directions	From Faro east on N125; IP1 exit 16 to Tavira; under archway, over r'bout & T-junc., right after church, following signs 'Centro Saude'. Right past army barracks, 1st left; 200m, fork right.

	Senhora Isabel Maria Castanho Paes
tel	+351 281 321573
mobile	+351 919 603256
fax	+351 281 325632
email	conventav@hotmail.com

B&B

Map 6 Entry 184

Pousada de Tavira - Convento da Graça

Rua D. Paio Peres Correia, 8800-407 Tavira, Algarve

It is a stunning building on a hilltop site, a conversion of a 16th-century convent in the Jewish quarter of Tavira. The convent of the cloistered Augustinian nuns was founded by King Sebastião in 1569, and its most striking features, apart from its gorgeous ochre façade, are its hushed cloisters and central staircase built in baroque style. There are even some archaeological traces of Islamic origin – now partially visible from the bar. The restaurant is formal but not too much so, the food is reasonably priced, the bar is cosy and softly lit, and the staff couldn't be nicer. Out in the lovely gardens is a large terrace with stunning views, and two excellent pools set into the lawns, one for children. Bedrooms are elegant and roomy, some in the cloister overlooking the town square. One of the suites has a mezzanine level so you can lounge in comfort and enjoy a quiet read, another has its own terrace and small garden. Pop into the Camera Obscura next door, hop into the car and drive up into the hills, stroll down to the beach, deserted and beautiful out of season. Special.

rooms	36: 7 doubles, 24 twins, 5 suites.
price	€150–€230. Suites €182. Special offers available - see web site.
meals	Lunch & dinner from €30.
closed	Never.
directions	Signed in Tavira.

Senhor João Portugal

tel	+351 218 442001
fax	+351 218 442085
email	recepcao.conventograca@pousadas.pt
web	www.pousadas.pt

Madeira

Quinta das Vinhas

Lombo dos Serrões - Est° Calheta, 9370-221 Calheta, Madeira

Stay at one of the oldest manor houses on the island. It is flanked by the mountains and has views that sweep over its vineyards to the blue sea. The 17th-century homestead — all flagstone floors, wooden ceilings and handpainted tiles — exudes tradition. The owner's family, of English origin, once ran the biggest sugar cane mill in Madeira. Now the dining room — where food and wines are delicious — is in the old kitchen, and the old prayer room is a reading room; both are adorned with elegant antiques. This peaceful and gracious atmosphere extends to the lush grounds, where you may stroll among the tulip trees and the angel's trumpets, and perhaps pluck a passion fruit or two. Then back for a glass of the Quinta's very fine madeira. Bedrooms in the main house have traditional furnishings and are flooded with light; the apartments, built of Madeiran stone, with minimalist interiors and bold colours, are set apart. Fish from the village pier, take a dip in the sea, surf the winter swell, visit the Chapel of the Three Kings. A fabulous place.

rooms	6 + 14: 6 doubles. 14 cottages for 2-3. Extra beds available.
price	€75-€100. Cottages from €560 per week.
meals	Dinner €15. Pool snacks available.
closed	Rarely.
directions	Thro' Lugar de Baixo, on to Ponte do Sol; exit at next 2 r'bouts for Calheta. Thro' 2 tunnels; at r'bout, exit for Prazeres. Right at 2nd sign for Est da Calheta. On for 0.8km, gate on right.

Isabel Welsh Talas

tel	+351 291 824086
fax	+351 291 822187
email	info@qdvmadeira.com
web	www.qdvmadeira.com

B&B & Self-catering

Map 5 Entry 186

Vila Afonso

Estrada João Gonçalves Zarco, 574-B, 9325-033 Estreito de Câmara de Lobos, Madeira

From high on the island's southern coast, the garden looks over an entrancing jumble of banana groves, vineyards and rooftops to the intense blue of the Atlantic far below. It's a view you won't forget. The family has been here for four generations but the mellow old stone building goes back to the 17th century. This is where guests stay (the Afonsos have built themselves a new house next door, on the other side of a lofty, glass-encased pool). The B&B rooms are traditional: shining wood, pastel walls, lush house plants and a few antiques. Beds range from wrought-iron to an elegant four-poster; bathrooms are spotless and new. The garden is equally irreproachable: statues are dotted around vivid lawns criss-crossed with paths and exotic plants. The family farm and vineyard cover just over one acre. Senhor Afonso is passionate about the production of Madeira wine and gives presentations and wine-tastings for guests each week. There's even a little taverna on site. If you prefer to self-cater, you can take one of the two bungalows behind the house.

rooms	6 + 2: 6 doubles.
	2 bungalows: 1 for 2, 1 for 4.
price	€60–€89.
meals	Restaurants 10-minute walk.
closed	Rarely.
directions	Take m'way from airport, then 2nd sign to Câmara de Lobos/Estreito de Câmara de Lobos, 5th exit. Right onto main street João Gonçalves Zarco. Follow signs for Estreito de Câmara de Lobos. Keep on road.

	Senhor João Afonso
tel	+351 291 911510
fax	+351 291 911515
email	info@vilaafonso.com
web	www.vilaafonso.com

B&B & Self-catering

Map 5 Entry 187

Quinta da Bela Vista

Caminho do Avista Navios, 4, , 9000-129 Funchal, Madeira

Stunning – a manor house with exquisite formal walled gardens and sweeping views of Funchal Bay. The quinta is not short of antiques, and bedrooms in the main house are classical with warm colours and traditional prints. Bathrooms are marble. Bedrooms in the new annexe are equally good, but with a modern feel; choose those in the main house for old-fashioned atmosphere. For morning privacy, ask for breakfast to be served on your private terrace. The main restaurant – yellow walls, black and white tiled floors – serves classy dishes at one big antique table; there's also à la carte. Hushed lounges have open fires in winter, there are a billiard room, card room, library and small fitness room with jacuzzi and sauna, and outside a tennis court and a pool. Relax with a drink or a snack from the bar and drink in those glorious views. If you prefer to go snorkelling or scuba diving, the friendly and charming staff will suggest local trips, and there's a small courtesy bus to and from Funchal. Or make the most of the hotel's yacht and drop in on the local islands. Bliss.

rooms	89: 82 twins/doubles, 7 suites.
price	€202-€448.
meals	Dinner, 3 courses, €38.
closed	Never.
directions	From Airport follow signs for Funchal; exit for S. Martinho. In village, left at next roundabout. 3rd road left, 'Caminho do Avista Navios'. Signed.

	Dr. Gonçalo Monteiro
tel	+351 291 706400
fax	+351 291 706401
email	info@belavistamadeira.com
web	www.belavistamadeira.com

Hotel

Map 5 Entry 188

Choupana Hills Resort

Travessa do Largo da Choupana, 9060-348 Funchal, Madeira

Be spoiled by this designer hotel with its sumptuous Portuguese-Asian twist.
A gold embossed wall-hanging above an open fire, a water bowl flickering with
tiny candles, vibrant armchairs — orange, lime, mulberry in the bar, plum and red
in the dining room — and vast, glass candle-holders. This new hotel is filled with
gorgeous antiques and modern things, its large lagoon-like pool is surrounded by
young gardens of cacti and palms, and you'll skip with pleasure when you discover
your luxurious bungalow on stilts... its exotic canopied wooden bed, its crisper-
than-crisp bedlinen, its rich polished floors, its private terrace with views of
Funchal bay. All the rooms feel private and peaceful, sparkling bathrooms have
lush goodies and thick bathrobes to lounge in, and the suites get outdoor jacuzzis.
Pad down to the spa where a medley of blissful treatments can be arranged, have a
steamy Turkish bath or take a dip in the serene indoor pool. Then afternoon tea in
the lounge, or a cocktail at the bar. Charming staff, fusion cuisine, tranquillity — a
hedonists' retreat.

rooms	63: 59 twins/doubles, 4 suites.
price	From €313.
meals	Lunch €30. Dinner, 3 courses, €40.
closed	Never.
directions	Follow the main road towards the Botanical Gardens. Follow signs to Choupana Hills.

	Senhor Philippe Moreau
tel	+351 291 206020
fax	+351 291 206021
email	info@choupanahills.com
web	www.choupanahills.com

Hotel

Map 5 Entry 189

Estalagem Quintinha São João

Rua da Levada de São João 4, 9000-191 Funchal , Madeira

Overhung by creepers and set in a curved stone wall, the tiles proclaiming the name of the hotel look deeply traditional. In fact, the place was built less than ten years ago. Once inside, there is a curious time shift; you can almost imagine yourself transported to the England of *Brief Encounter*. Everything is immaculate and welcoming but there's an old-world formality about the public rooms: brass lamps with pleated shades on occasional tables, gleaming antique desks, gilt-framed oil paintings, velvet-covered armchairs, carefully placed pieces of good china, a grand piano... Each of the understated, luxurious bedrooms has its own sitting area and some charming local touches – carved wooden bedheads and pieces of island embroidery – and breakfast in the restaurant (hot or cold buffet) is at tables covered with snowy cloths. Out in the big sub-tropical gardens, the lawns are punctuated with palms, ferns and wrought-iron seats; flowers spill from terracotta urns and hydrangeas bloom in the shelter of low stone walls.

rooms	43: 34 twins, 9 suites.
price	€145–€175. Suites €173–€232. Singles €103.
meals	Dinner €30.
closed	Never.
directions	From airport towards Funchal & Ribeira Brava. Exit 9 on left. At r'bout 3rd exit, thro' tunnel to r'bout; exit to go back way you came following signs for hospital. Back thro' tunnel, right after Hotel São João; after 25m on right.

	Senhor André Barreto
tel	+351 291 740920
fax	+351 291 740928
email	abarreto@quintinhasaojoao.com
web	www.quintinhasaojoao.com

Hotel

Map 5 Entry 190

Quinta das Eiras

Sítio da Achada das Eiras, St. António da Serra, 9100-266 Santa Cruz, Madeira

Against the far-off backdrop of a wooded mountain ridge is a scattering of little chalet bungalows standing on stilts. Separated by tree ferns, lawns and flowerbeds, surrounded by trees and shrubs, they have an almost fairytale appearance; each is reached via a narrow wooden staircase to its veranda. Inside, a simple bed/sitting room plus a kitchenette and a basic shower, all presented in a delightfully rustic-contemporary style. The walls are panelled with golden wood; the floors and the furniture are of a darker, richer hue. All are designed for two but a couple of them combine to accommodate four. However, limited space means these chalets are more suitable for couples than turbo-charged children. Old apple trees decorate the one-acre garden and a curved swimming pool sits prettily in a velvety lawn. Also for self-caterers is the more soberly furnished apartment in the main house, and a red-shuttered stone cottage with a deep veranda amongst the trees; both would be perfect for two. Sr and Sra Gomes are affable, talkative hosts, and live on the spot. *Minimum stay two nights.*

rooms	7: 3 chalets for 2, 2 for 4. Apartment for 2. Cottage for 2.
price	€80–€90 for 2. €160 for 4.
meals	Self-catering.
closed	Never.
directions	From airport towards Santo da Serra. Left after town square, on towards Quinta das Eiras. NB: there are no signs for Quinta on main road.

	Senhor Luis Mendes Gomes
tel/fax	+351 291 552511
mobile	+351 966 306325
email	quintadaseiras@mail.net4b.pt
web	www.wonderfulland.com/eiras

Self-catering

Map 5 Entry 191

Recommended reading

Two stalwarts of Portuguese literature are Luis de Camoes, Portugal's bard, and Fernando Pessoa. Camoes has a public holiday dedicated to him and his classic work is *The Lusiads*. Pessoa - born in 1888 - wrote hundreds of volumes of poetry and the famous *The Book of Disquiet* before he died in 1935.

Eça de Queiroz is the major voice of realism in 19th-century Portuguese literature and is best known for *The Maias*, a tale of the destruction of a dissolute aristocratic Portuguese family in the 1800s. *The Illustrious House of Ramirez* and *The Relic* are his, too.

Lobo Antunes, a psychologist /writer, has built his prize-winning career on solid rocks such as *Elephant's Memory* and *Inquisitors' Manual*; he often draws on his experiences as a soldier in the Angolan War.

Portugal's answer to Gabriel Garçia Marquez is Jose Saramago. His is a highly original voice, using a mixture of history and fantasy and he sets a unique rhythm that uses minimal punctuation. Try *Baltazar and Blimunda*, *The Year of the Death of Ricardo Reis*, and *The History of the Siege of Lisbon*. After many years in exile, Saramago returned to write *Journey to Portugal*, a commentary on the psyche of the Portuguese.

For entertaining history try Richard Zimler who combines a career as a novelist with teaching. *The Last Kabbalist of Lisbon*, *Guardian of the Dawn*, and *Hunting Midnight* follow the lives of a Portuguese Jewish family and are steeped in history.

A worthy mention goes to Marion Kaplan's *The Portuguese - The Land and Its People*. Updated in 2006, this informative and entertaining book includes the history, sites, culture and customs of a warm and wonderful people.

Linda Taylor Gonçalves
Proprietor, The Griffin International Bookshop, Almancil, Algarve
www.griffinbookshop.com

Where on the web?

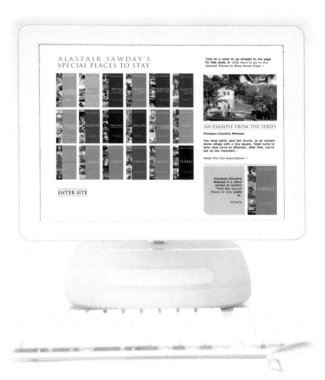

The World Wide Web is big – very big. So big, in fact, that it can be a fruitless search if you don't know where to find reliable, trustworthy, up-to-date information about fantastic places to stay in Europe, India, Morocco and beyond....

Fortunately, there's www.specialplacestostay.com, where you can dip into all of our guides, find special offers from owners, catch up on news about the series and tell us about the special places you've been to.

www.specialplacestostay.com

Discover your perfect self-catering escape in Britain... With the same punch and attitude as all our printed guides, Special Escapes celebrates only those places we have visited and genuinely like.

www.special-escapes.co.uk

Order form

All these books are available in major bookshops or you may order them direct.
Post and packaging are FREE within the UK.

British Hotels, Inns & Other Places	£14.99
British Bed & Breakfast	£14.99
British Bed & Breakfast for Garden Lovers	£14.99
Croatia	£11.99
French Bed & Breakfast	£15.99
French Holiday Homes	£12.99
French Hotels, Châteaux & Other Places	£14.99
Greece	£11.99
Green Places to Stay	£13.99
India	£11.99
Ireland	£12.99
Italy	£14.99
London	£9.99
Morocco	£11.99
Mountains of Europe	£9.99
Paris Hotels	£10.99
Portugal	£11.99
Pubs & Inns of England & Wales	£14.99
Spain	£14.99
Turkey	£11.99
One Planet Living	**£4.99**
The Little Food Book	£6.99
The Little Money Book	£6.99
Six Days	£12.99

Please make cheques payable to Alastair Sawday Publishing   Total £

Please send cheques to: Alastair Sawday Publishing, The Old Farmyard, Yanley
Lane, Long Ashton, Bristol BS41 9LR. For credit card orders call 01275 395431
or order directly from our web site **www.specialplacestostay.com**

Title   First name   Surname

Address

Postcode   Tel

If you do not wish to receive mail from other like-minded companies, please tick here ☐
If you would prefer not to receive information about special offers on our books, please tick here ☐

Report form

If you have any comments on entries in this guide, please let us have them.
If you have a favourite house, hotel, inn or other new discovery, please let us
know about it. You can return this form, email info@sawdays.co.uk, or visit
www.specialplacestostay.com and click on 'contact'.

Existing entry
Property name:_____

Entry number: _____ Date of visit: ___ / ___ / ___

New recommendation
Property name:_____

Address: _____

_____

Tel: _____

Your comments
What did you like (or dislike) about this place? Were the people friendly?
What was the location like? What sort of food did they serve?

_____

_____

_____

_____

_____

_____

_____

_____

Your details
Name: _____

Address: _____

Postcode: _____ Tel: _____

Please send completed form to ASP, The Old Farmyard, Yanley Lane,
Long Ashton, Bristol BS41 9LR

Quick reference indices

Wheelchair accessible
At least one bedroom and bathroom accessible for wheelchair users.
Phone for details.

Minho • 1 • 8 • 19
Douro • 23
Trás-os-Montes • 37
Beira • 44 • 50 • 54 • 62
Estremadura • 70 • 77 • 83 • 84 • 86 • 94 • 101 •
Ribatejo • 103 • 104 • 105
Alentejo • 122 • 128 • 134 • 138 • 146
Algarve • 156 • 178
Madeira • 188

No car
Places within 10 miles of a coach or train station and the owners can pick you up

Minho 2 • 3 • 5 • 7 • 8 • 10 • 12 • 16 • 17 • 18 • 19
Douro • 22 • 23 • 26 • 27 • 28 • 30 • 32 • 33 • 34 • 35
Trás-os-Montes • 36 • 38 • 39
Beira • 41 • 42 • 43 • 44 • 46 • 47 • 49 • 50 • 52 • 57 • 59 • 60 • 63 • 65 •
Estremadura • 66 • 67 • 68 • 71 • 73 • 74 • 75 • 77 • 78 • 79 • 81 • 84 • 86 • 87 • 89 • 92 • 93 • 95 • 97 • 99 • 100 • 101
Ribatejo 103 • 104 • 106 • 107 • 108
Alentejo • 110 • 115 • 117 • 120 • 121 • 122 • 123 • 124 • 129 • 132 • 133 •

134 • 136 • 137 • 139 • 140 • 142 • 144 • 146 •
Algarve • 149 • 154 • 155 • 156 • 157 • 158 • 160 • 162 • 163 • 164 • 167 • 169 • 170 • 171 • 172 • 173 • 174 • 175 • 181 • 182 • 183 • 184
Madeira • 188 • 189

Bike
Bikes are available on the premises to hire or borrow

Minho • 3 • 5 • 6 • 7 • 10 • 17 • 19
Douro • 23 • 24 • 25 • 27 • 32 • 34 • 35
Trás-os-Montes • 36 • 37 • 38 • 39
Beira • 41 • 42 • 45 • 46 • 48 • 49 • 51 • 52 • 55 • 63
Estremadura • 70 • 71 • 78 • 80 • 81 • 84 • 86 • 101 •
Ribatejo • 103 • 104 • 107
Alentejo • 109 • 113 • 115 • 117 • 118 • 119 • 120 • 122 • 123 • 124 • 127 • 129 • 131 • 132 • 133 • 134 • 136 • 137 • 138 • 139 • 140 • 142 • 143 • 144 • 145 • 146 • 147 •
Algarve • 148 • 149 • 152 • 155 • 156 • 157 • 158 • 162 • 164 • 165 • 167 • 169 • 170 • 173 • 174 • 175 • 180 • 181 • 182 • 183
Madeira • 191

Singles
These places have at least one single room or charge

half the double room rate
for single occupancy

Minho • 3 • 5 • 6 • 7 • 10
• 17 • 19
Douro • 23 • 24 • 25 • 27 •
32 • 34 • 35
Trás-os-Montes • 36 • 37 •
38 • 39
Beira • 41 • 42 • 45 • 46 •
48 • 49 • 51 • 52 • 55 • 63
Estremadura • 70 • 71 • 78
• 80 • 81 • 84 • 86 • 101
Ribatejo • 103 • 104 • 107
Alentejo • 109 • 113 • 115
• 117 • 118 • 119 • 120 •
122 • 123 • 124 • 127 •
129 • 131 • 132 • 133 •
134 • 136 • 137 • 138 •
139 • 140 • 142 • 143 •
144 • 145 • 146 • 147 •
Algarve • 148 • 149 • 152 •
155 • 156 • 157 • 158 •
162 • 164 • 165 • 167 •
169 • 170 • 173 • 174 •
175 • 180 • 181 • 182 •
183
Madeira • 191

Wine production
Places of particular interest
to wine buffs

Minho • 3 • 5 • 6 • 9 • 10
• 13 • 17 • 18 • 20
Douro 23 • 25 • 27 • 31 •
33 • 35
Trás-os-Montes • 36 • 37 •
41 • 46 • 47 • 49 • 64
Estremadura • 72
Alentejo • 110 • 113 • 149
• 155 • 162 • 169 •
Madeira • 186 • 187

Pool
These places have a
swimming pool on the
premises

Minho • 3 • 5 • 6 • 7 • 9 •
10 • 11 • 12 • 13 • 15 • 16
• 17 • 18 • 19 • 20
Douro • 23 • 25 • 27 • 28 •
29 • 30 • 31 • 32 • 34 • 35
Trás-os-Montes • 36 • 37 •
38 • 39
Beira • 42 • 43 • 45 • 46 •
48 • 49 • 50 • 53 • 54 • 56
• 58 • 60 • 62 • 63 • 64 •
65
Estremadura • 66 • 70 • 71
• 72 • 73 • 75 • 77 • 78 •
79 • 80 • 81 • 82 • 83 • 84
• 89 • 98 • 100 • 101 •
Ribatejo • 102 • 103 • 104
• 105 • 107 • 108 •
Alentejo • 109 • 111 • 113 •
114 • 115 • 117 • 118 • 119
• 120 • 121 • 122 • 123 •
124 • 125 • 126 • 127 •
128 • 129 • 130 • 132 •
133 • 134 • 135 • 136 •
137 • 138 • 139 • 142 •
143 • 144 • 146 • 147 •
Algarve • 148 • 149 • 150 •
151 • 153 • 154 • 155 •
156 • 157 • 158 • 159 •
160 • 161 • 162 • 163 •
164 • 165 • 166 • 167 •
168 • 169 • 170 • 171 •
172 • 173 • 174 • 175 •
176 • 177 • 178 • 179 •
180 • 181 • 182 • 183 •
184 • 185
Madeira • 186 • 187 • 188
• 189 • 190 • 191

Quick reference indices

Index by property name

Hotel Albatroz	84	Pousada de Óbidos/Castelo	69
Hotel Britânia	87	Pousada de Ourém/Fátima	102
Hotel Convento de São Paulo	122	Pousada de Queluz/Lisboa	85
Hotel Lisboa Plaza	88	Pousada de Sagres	153
Hotel Métropole	95	Pousada de Santa Clara-a-Velha	147
Hotel Residencial Casa do Outeiro	62	Pousada de Santiago de Cacém	138
Hotel Rural Horta da Moura	133	Pousada de Setúbal	99
Hotel rural Quinta da Geía	54	Pousada de Sousel	118
Inn Albergeria Bica-Boa	150	Pousada de Tavira	185
La Hoja de Roble	40	Pousada de Valença do Minho	1
Monte da Bravura	156	Pousada de Vila Nova de Cerveira	2
Monte da Moita Nova	143	Pousada de Vila Pouca da Beira	50
Monte das Cortelhas	169	Pousada de Vila Viçosa	128
Monte do Casal	176	Pousada do Alvito	135
Monte do Papa Léguas	144	Pousada do Crato	109
Monte dos Pensamentos	123	Pousada do Gerês-Caniçada/S. Bento	11
Monte Maravilhas	142	Pousada do Marão/São Gonçalo	24
Monte Rosa	155	Quinta Azenha do Ramalho	116
Monte Saraz	132	Quinta da Alfarrobeira	159
Monte Velho Nature Resort	152	Quinta da Bela Vista	188
Mouraria	96	Quinta da Bouça d'Arques	5
Na Curva do Rio	163	Quinta da Cebola Vermelha	170
Pedras Verdes Guesthouse	177	Quinta da Dourada	115
Pensão Avenida	22	Quinta da Espada	120
Pensão Residencial Sintra	73	Quinta da Fonte Bispo	181
Pomar Velho	113	Quinta da Lua	180
Pousada da Murtosa-Torreira/Ria	45	Quinta da Mata	38
Pousada de Alcácer do Sal	101	Quinta da Moenda	53
Pousada de Amares	12	Quinta da Pindella	17
Pousada de Arraiolos	119	Quinta da Ra	179
Pousada de Beja	137	Quinta da Saimeira	111
Pousada de Belmonte	56	Quinta da Timpeira	35
Pousada de Bragança	39	Quinta da Vila Francelina	46
Pousada de Estremoz	124	Quinta das Achadas	158
Pousada de Évora/Lóios	121	Quinta das Eiras	191
Pousada de Guimarães	19	Quinta das Lágrimas	58
Pousada de Manteigas	55	Quinta das Mestras	52
Pousada de Marvão/Santa Maria	112	Quinta das Sequóias	75
Pousada de Mesão Frio	29	Quinta das Vinhas	186

Index by property name

Index by place name

Index by place name

How to use this book

① Estremadura

Há Mar Ao Luar

Casa do Mar e Moinho do Luar, Alto S. Filipe CCI3114, 2900-300 Setúbal, Estremadura

② The vibrant Brazilian dancers in the paintings sum it up: this place is fun. And funky and charming. Stay in the windmill whose staircase, hugging the curved wall, winds romantically up from the circular living space to bed. Or take the beach cabana -- French windows pull the sea views into the open-plan bedroom/dining room downstairs, there are twin beds in the attic (reached by ladder) for the children and colourful ribbons hanging from the doors. It's the kind of place where you won't mind getting sand everywhere. Happy summer holidays will be spent here and everything has been designed with the sea in mind -- pictures of lighthouses, colourful tiling on the bathroom floors, hanging rails for tea towels, updside-down painted fish and buckets, whale-tail door handles, lobster pots and more. Breakfast waits in the fridge, fresh bread is attached to the door in the morning. White-sand views, peace, sea air -- inspirational. Pretty gardens too and a lovely pool to cool off in. It's good value and you're very close to beautiful beaches, dolphins, boat trips -- and, of course, the city.

③ rooms	1 + 5: 1 twin. Windmill for 2; house for 2; beach cabana for 2-4; 2 apartments for 2.	
④ price	€50-€90. Windmill €100-€120. Cabana, house & apts €75-€90.	
⑤ meals	Breakfast provided. Restaurants 1.5km.	
⑥ closed	Rarely.	
⑦ directions	From A2 for Setúbal centre; follow signs for Pousada de São Filipe. Up hill until sign for Há Mar auo Luar; 2nd on right.	

Senhora Maria Pereira Caldas

tel   +351 265 220901
fax   +351 265 534432
email   hamaraoluar@iol.pt
web   www.hamaraoluar.com

⑨ B&B & Self-catering

⑧ Map 3 Entry 100